How to expand ;
your |

by

R. A. Penfold

BERNARD BABANI (publishing) LTD
THE GRAMPIANS
SHEPHERDS BUSH ROAD
LONDON W6 7N
ENGLAND

Please Note

Although every care has been taken with the production of this book to ensure that any projects, designs, modifications and/or programs, etc., contained herewith, operate in a correct and safe manner and also that any components specified are normally available in Great Britain, the Publishers and Author(s) do not accept responsibility in any way for the failure (including fault in design) of any projects, design, modification or program to work correctly or to cause damage to any equipment that it may be connected to or used in conjunction with, or in respect of any other damage or injury that may be so caused, nor do the Publishers accept responsibility in any way for the failure to obtain specified components.

Notice is also given that if equipment that is still under warranty is modified in any way or used or connected with home-built equipment then that warranty may be void.

First Published – November 1998

British Library Cataloguing in Publication Data
A catalogue record for this book is available from the British Library

ISBN 0 85934 450 9

Cover Designed by Gregor Arthur
Printed and Bound in Great Britain by Cox & Wyman Ltd, Reading

Preface

Since its introduction in 1981 the IBM PC has undergone continuous changes and developments. In general, IBM themselves have led the way, but in recent times the various "clone" manufacturers have introduced some innovations of their own. Despite all the improvements that have been made, and the increased capabilities of modern PCs, a PC still remains very much a PC. Software and most add-ons for the original machines will still function perfectly well in a modern PC. A factor that has certainly aided the popularity of PCs is their open architecture. IBM published the full specification of the PC expansion slots, making it easy for third party suppliers to produce and sell PC expansion cards of various types. This has led to numerous specialist add-ons for the PC being produced, as well as a good range of mainstream products. PCs and their interfaces have moved on over the years, but there are still numerous add-ons available that enable PCs to work well in numerous everyday and specialist applications.

While expanding a PC is, in the main, a reasonably straightforward affair, there are inevitably some complications to most aspects of PC upgrading. The main purpose this book is first to explain the basics of PC hardware, and then to help untangle the difficulties that can arise when undertaking the more popular of PC upgrades. The topics covered include floppy and hard disc drives, memory expansion, display adapters and monitors, CD-ROMs and soundcards, ports, and keyboards.

Many PC users prefer, as far as possible, to do their own maintenance and this subject is covered in chapter 5. Assembling your own PC might seem to be a rather ambitious task, but the modular construction of these computers means that it is in fact much easier than one might expect to put together a PC to exactly meet your desired specification. With all the necessary parts for a PC now being readily available, this is an increasingly popular way of obtaining a PC, and one that is described in the final chapter of this book. If building a PC "from scratch" is too daunting, chapter 6 tells you how to upgrade an old PC into a "new" one having a modern specification.

R. A. Penfold

Contents

Other Titles of Interest

Trademarks

MS-DOS Windows 95 and Windows 98 are registered trademarks of Microsoft Corporation

IBM PC, XT, AT, PS/2, OS/2 and PC-DOS are registered trademarks of International Business Machines Corporation

Pentium, Celeron, and Xeon are registered trademarks of Intel Corporation

X2 Technology is a registered trademark of US Robotics Corporation

K6-2 3D Now! is a registered trademark of Advanced Micro Design (AMD)

K56 Flex is a registered trademark of Lucent Technology Inc. Rockwell Corporation

Chapter 1

PC OVERVIEW

The are many possible reasons for the unrivalled popularity of the IBM PCs and the numerous compatible machines, which have been the standard business microcomputer for many years now. One contributory factor is certainly their enormous expansion potential. The basic computer, or "system unit" as it is generally called, is unusable on its own. It requires the addition of disc drives, a monitor, a keyboard, and even such things as an add-on display generator before it will provide any useful function. This modular approach has been the cause of a certain amount of criticism, but in truth it is a very good way of doing things.

If all you require is a very basic computer with an inexpensive processor, a hard disc drive of modest capacity and a small monitor for text use, then you can buy a PC of that type. You do not need to spend money on expensive disc hard drives, up-market processors, or large monitors that you do not need or want. If, on the other hand, you are interested in graphics applications and require high-resolution true-colour graphics plus a large and fast hard disc drive, you will have a choice of several PC compatible systems that offer a suitable specification. With requirements for computer systems that fall somewhere between these two extremes you are likely to be spoiled for choice, with a vast number of suitable systems to choose from. If you can not find something that exactly meets your requirements, then it is possible to buy a basic computer system and add in suitable peripherals yourself. Due to IBM's so-called "open architecture" policy (publishing full technical details of their microcomputers so that third party manufacturers can produce add-ons for them), the range of add-on boards and other peripherals for the PC series runs into many hundreds. Some PC suppliers will actually build a PC to your specifications.

In this book we will mainly be concerned with the hardware side of PC compatible computing. In this first chapter we will take a look at PC hardware in general, going into any great detail on some subjects, but considering others in a superficial manner. Subsequent chapters provide detailed information on several topics not fully discussed in this chapter (disc drives, display cards, etc.). Those who are already familiar with the general principles of PC hardware and expansion will probably be familiar with some of the topics covered in chapter 1. Readers in this category might like to skip over some sections of this chapter. Those who are not familiar with PC hardware should study this chapter in some detail before progressing to any of the other chapters that cover a topic of particular interest to them. Trying to expand a PC without understanding the differences between the various types of PC and their general make up could easily lead to some costly mistakes.

Software Compatibility

The term "software compatibility" in a PC context originally referred to the ability (or lack of it) to run standard IBM PC software designed to operate under either the PC-DOS or MS-DOS operating systems. These two operating systems can for virtually all practical purposes be regarded as inter-changeable. PC-DOS was the operating system produced by Microsoft for use with real IBM PCs, whereas MS-DOS is the version for compatibles. In theory, any software written to run under PC/MS-DOS should run on any computer that has either of these operating systems up and running properly. In practice there is a complication in that much software sometimes controls the computer's hardware by reading from it and writing to it directly, rather than going through the operating system.

The problem here is that any variations in the hardware are supposed to be handled by the operating system. If data is written to a printer port, the operating system should ensure that the data is sent to the right piece of hardware, and that the flow of data to the printer is controlled properly. If data is sent direct to the hardware by the program, and it monitors the hardware directly to see if the printer is ready to receive data, there is a risk of incompatibility. In these circumstances the program will only run properly if the computer has the right peripheral components at the right places in the computer's input/output map. The operating system will not be involved in the exchange of data, and will not intervene to ensure that it all goes smoothly.

In days gone by quite a large number of programs relied on direct control of the hardware in order to achieve a suitably fast operating speed. This made it important to have hardware that accurately mimicked a genuine IBM PC. Of course, these days it is compatibility with Windows 95 and 98 that it of more importance and basic MS-DOS compatibility is something we now take for granted. Software drivers integrate hardware such as video boards and pointing devices with Windows (any version), and it is these drivers that ensure a modern PC is fully compatible. Odd compatibility problems do still arise from time to time, but obtaining updated software drivers for the offending piece of hardware should sort things out.

ROM BIOS

An important factor for good compatibility is the quality of the ROM BIOS. ROM stands for "read only memory", and it is a component (or two in the case of some AT type computers) which contains a computer program. This program contains the BIOS, or "basic input/output system." The first function of the BIOS is to run a few diagnostic checks at switch-on to ensure that the computer is up and running properly. It then looks on the disc drives in search of the operating system, which it then loads into the computer's memory. The operating system then takes over, but the BIOS contains software routines that can be utilized by the operating system.

You will often encounter the term "booting" or "booting-up", which refers to this process of the operating system being automatically loaded from disc and run. This term is derived from the fact that operating system appears to load itself into the computer's memory, which is akin to pulling ones self up by ones bootlaces. Of course, the operating system only appears to be loading and running itself. The truth of the matter is that routines in the ROM BIOS are carrying out this process.

The software in the BIOS, or "firmware" as programs in this form is often termed, must not be an exact copy of the IBM original due to copyright restrictions. Things have moved on, and a modern BIOS has to deal more hardware parameters than the original BIOS was designed to cope with anyway. Several companies produce BIOS chips that do the same basic job as the IBM original, but by a different means so that copyright problems are avoided. Obviously this gives rise to the possibility of incompatibilities, but any modern BIOS should be well tried and tested. Again, I have used many IBM compatibles over the years, using BIOS chips from manufacturers including Phoenix, Award, and AMI, and have yet to encounter any incompatibility problems.

Probably the most likely cause of software incompatibility these days is simply not having a PC that is up to the task. The best modern PCs must be something like a thousand times faster than the originals, and have several hundred times more memory. Modern software mostly requires a PC that has a modern specification, and with the more demanding programs a very high specification is required. The much given advice of buy the software that suits your requirements first and then the buy hardware to suit it afterwards, remains as good as it ever was. It is as well to bear in mind that there is almost always a significant gap between new "improved" hardware arriving on the scene, and software being updated to take advantage of it. The widespread use of Windows has eased this problem, and new hardware should be supplied complete with Windows drivers. Even so, with the more advanced items of hardware there can still be a gap between its launch and the arrival of widespread software support.

PC Versions
The PCs and compatibles have evolved over a period of several years, and the more up-market systems in use today have specifications that bear little resemblance to the original IBM

PC, which was launched in 1981. The original had just 64K of memory, a monochrome text only display, and included a cassette port. The IBM compatible I am using to produce the text and drawings for this book has a 64 megabyte (65536K) of RAM, a colour graphics board and monitor that can handle up to 1600 by 1200 pixels with 16 million colours, plus a 32X CD-ROM drive and a 4.3 gigabyte fast hard disc. It also uses a microprocessor that renders it more than a hundred times faster than the original PC. Despite this, it is still highly compatible with the original computer. It can almost certainly run any software that will run on the original version of the computer, and can take practically any expansion card that is compatible with the original machine.

The opposite is not true though, and there is much software and a lot of expansion cards that will work in my PC, but are unusable with the original computer (and many of the more recent compatibles come to that). It is worth briefly considering basic details of the various versions of the IBM PC range. This is not just a matter of historical interest, but because it can be helpful to know how your particular machine fits into the overall scheme of things.

Original PCs
The "PC" in IBM PC merely stands for "personal computer". This is a possible cause of confusion since the IBM PCs and compatibles are often referred to simply as "PCs", but this is also a general term for any microcomputer which is primarily intended for business rather than home use. Anyway, in this book the term "PC" will only be used to refer to the IBM PC family of computers and the many compatible machines.

The original PC had relatively limited expansion potential. It had facilities for five full-length expansion slots, but this was not quite as good as it might at first appear. With a maximum of only 256K RAM on the main circuit board, (64K on the earliest PCs), and slots being required for disc controllers, serial and parallel ports, and the display card, some of these slots were required to provide essential functions. To ease the problem, several manufacturers produced multi-function cards, which gave such things as an extra 384K of memory, plus serial and parallel ports all on one card. This was more than a little helpful at the time, but with modern PCs this sort of thing is unnecessary, because the standard interfaces are included on the main board.

The main problem when trying to expand an early PC was often the power supply. This had a rating of 63.5 watts, which is low in comparison to the ratings of around 150 watts for the later versions, and 230 watts for a modern PC. 63.5 watts was actually quite a hefty power supply for a microcomputer of the time, but it nevertheless provided little more power than the basic system required, and little more than many modern microprocessors consume. Anything more than the addition of one or two low power cards required the fitting of a more beefy power supply unit, which usually meant a 150 watt type, as fitted to some later versions of the PC, and most early PC compatibles. Upgrading an early PC is not a worthwhile proposition these days, and the original PCs are now entering the realms of collector's items.

PC XT

IBM introduced the PC XT in 1983, and it is this model rather than the original PC that tends to be considered as the first "real" PC. The "XT" part of the name is an abbreviation for extended, incidentally. It was an improvement on the original design in a number of ways. One of the improvements was the ability to have up to 640K of socketed RAM on the main circuit board, or "motherboard" as it is usually termed. The original PCs had all the RAM chips soldered directly to the board, making it difficult and expensive to replace a faulty chip. With the ability to have 640K of RAM on the motherboard, which is the maximum that the design of the computer permits, there was no need to take up an expansion slot with a memory board if you need the full complement of RAM.

The expansion slot problem was eased anyway, by the inclusion of no less than eight slots on the motherboard. Even with slots occupied by disc controllers, serial and parallel ports, and a display board, there would still typically be four or five slots left for more exotic peripherals. Two of the slots are only suitable for short expansion boards. This is simply due to physical limitations, with a disc drive preventing full-length cards from being fitted into these two slots. This was not a major drawback since many expansion cards were (and are) of the half-length variety. It was not inconceivable that users would wish to have seven or eight full-length boards in an XT, but this was a highly unlikely state of affairs. However, some compatibles were capable of taking eight full-length cards. The 135-watt fan cooled power supply (usually 150 watts on clones) enabled plenty of peripherals to be powered without any risk of overloading the supply unit. Originally the XT was supplied complete with a 10-megabyte hard disc drive, but this was later made an optional extra. A 20-megabyte hard drive option was also available.

Turbo PCs

The computers in the IBM PC family are all based on microprocessors from the Intel 8086 series of microprocessors. The PC and PC XT computers are based on 8088, which is a slightly simplified version of the 8086. Whereas the 8086 processor has 16 pins which carry data into and out of the device, the 8088 has only eight pins for this purpose. This means that the 8088 has to take in and put out 16-bit chunks of data or program instructions as two 8-bit chunks ("bytes"), one after the other. This is undesirable as it slows down the computer to a significant degree. Coupled with the relatively slow clock speed used in the PC and PC XT of just 4.77MHz, this meant that the standard PCs had little more computing power than the faster 8-bit computers of the time. It could be argued that the XT class PCs were in fact eight-bit computers and not "real" 16-bit types. By current standards they are very slow computers, and like the original PCs are now collector's items.

IBM never produced what could really be regarded as a "turbo" version of the PC or PC XT. Most PC clones were and are of this type, although modern PCs have developed to the point where the "turbo" name is no longer adequate to describe them. In the early days of "turbo" PCs there were three basic routes to obtaining increased speed. These could be used singly or in any combination. Details of the three methods are given below.

1. Increased Clock Speed

The most obvious way of obtaining increased operating speed is to use a higher clock frequency. It is an oversimplification to say that doubling the clock frequency of the processor doubles the speed of the computer, but in practice this is more or less what happens. In order to use a higher clock frequency successfully the microprocessor must obviously be able to run reliably at the higher frequency, as must the memory chips and other circuits in the computer. Alternatively, the processor can operate at full speed, with the other circuits operating more slowly. The processor has so-called "wait states" to slow things down and let the rest of the hardware catch up.

2. Using an 8086 Microprocessor

Using the 8086 with its 16-bit data bus might seem an obvious way of getting improved performance, but matters are not as simple as it might at first appear. The early PCs had 8-bit expansion slots, making it difficult to obtain full hardware compatibility with them if the 16-bit 8086 was used. This problem was not insurmountable, and some 8086 based compatibles (notably some Amstrad and Olivetti machines) were produced. This method of performance boosting was a relatively rare one though.

3. Using the NEC V20

The NEC V20 microprocessor was capable of undertaking all 8088 instructions, and was fully compatible with it. The point about the V20 is that compared with the 8088 it took fewer clock pulses to complete some instructions. This obviously gave a boost in speed, but not a vast one. From my experience and tests I would say that the increase was somewhere in the region of 20% to 30%. There was a V30 microprocessor, which was a streamlined version of the 8086. Although we are now used to PCs fitted with non-Intel processors, for many years the V20 and V30 were the only compatible processors available.

PC AT Computers

Rather than trying to speed up the PC and PC XT, IBM produced what was effectively a completely new design, but one which largely maintained software and hardware compatibility with the PC and PC XT. This computer was the PC AT, and the "AT" part of the name stands for "advanced technology." This was based on the Intel 80286 microprocessor, which is an improved version of the 8086. Like the 8086 it has a 16-bit data bus, and the AT was therefore a true 16-bit computer. The AT achieves higher operating speeds than the PC and PC XT because it operates at a higher clock speed. The original AT operated at 6MHz, but the later versions had an 8MHz clock. Comparing the speed of the PC and PC XT computers with the AT models is difficult since the 80286 takes fewer clock cycles per instruction than the 8086 or 8088. Thus, while it might seem as though a 10MHz XT compatible was faster than a 6MHz or 8MHz AT, this is not actually the case. Popular methods of speed testing generally put the AT many times faster than the original 4.77MHz PC and PC XT machines. If you take the clock speed of an AT in MHz, then it is roughly that many times faster than a 4.77MHz XT, according to the popular speed test programs anyway.

The original IBM AT computers were fitted with 512K of RAM on the motherboard, but later compatible machines were able to take the full 640K on the motherboard. In fact most AT computers could take at least 1 megabyte of memory on the main circuit board, and many were equipped to take 4 or 8 megabytes. These large amounts of RAM are made possible by an extra operating mode of the 80286 which takes advantage of extra address lines on the chip. However, when running PC/MS-DOS software the 80286 can not directly use the RAM above the 640K limit. This is not to say that there is no point in having the extra RAM. Some programs can use it in slightly roundabout methods, such as using the RAM for a disc cache or a RAM disc. Also, operating systems such as OS/2 and Windows can run programs in the mode that takes full advantage of the whole 16-megabyte address range.

As it was a true 16-bit computer, in order to take full advantage of the 16-bit data bus the AT needed to have 16-bit expansion slots. This obviously raised possibilities with incompatibility between the AT and existing 8-bit PC expansion cards. In order to minimise these problems the 16-bit expansion slots of the AT and subsequent PCs are in the form of standard 8-bit slots plus a second connector which carries the extra lines needed by 16-bit expansion boards. This means that any 8-bit card should work in an AT style computer, with the only exception of boards that are PC or PC XT specific for some other reason. The only common example of this that springs to mind are the PC and PC XT hard disc controller cards. These have their own BIOS, whereas an AT hard disc controller card makes use of routines in the main BIOS on the motherboard. This gives what is really a firmware compatibility problem, rather than what could strictly speaking be termed hardware incompatibility. There were actually some boards, such as certain 16-bit VGA display cards, that would work in either type of computer. They sometimes achieved this by detecting electronically which type of computer they were fitted in, and then configuring themselves accordingly. In other cases the user had to set a switch on the card to the appropriate position. In most cases though, 16-bit cards are incompatible with PC and PC XT machines.

AT computers, even those using the faster versions of the 80286 chip, are now well and truly obsolete. If still in good order they will quite happily run contemporary software, but there are no practical upgrades that will bring one of these computers up to a specification that is suitable for running modern software. So much of the original PC would have to be replaced that you would effectively be building a new computer.

80386 ATs

When Intel produced an improved version of the 80286 microprocessor, the 80386, it was inevitable that this device would soon be used in a new and faster generation of PCs. However, IBM never produced an 80386-based version of the PC. IBM has produced computers based on this microprocessor, but not in a straightforward PC guise. The IBM "PS/2" range used a different form of expansion bus, and it is discussed in more detail later on in this chapter. This lack of an IBM 80386 based PC to clone meant that the clone manufacturers were left without any standards to follow when producing 80386 PCs. Computers of this type are effectively AT clones, but using the 80386 plus its support chips instead of the 80286 and the relevant devices. Modern PCs are developments of the 80386 AT style computers. Although they have developed almost beyond recognition, modern PCs are still AT class PCs.

Using the 80386 in an AT style computer does have some advantages. The 80386 can operate with clock rates of up to 33MHz, or 40MHz for some 80386 compatible chips. I have often seen it stated that the 80386 performs instructions in fewer clock cycles than the 80286, giving a vast increase in performance. On the other hand, the results of speed tests on various 80286 and 80386 computers would seem to suggest that there is little to choose between the two types of computer when running at the same clock rate. The 80386 is a 32-bit microprocessor, which makes it potentially more powerful in maths intensive applications than the 16-bit 80286. However, to take advantage of this it is necessary to have software that is written specifically for the 32-bit 80386. These days we take 32-bit operating systems and applications software for granted, but when the 80386 first came along there was relatively little software that could fully exploit its potential.

Apart from its ability to access memory 32 bits at a time, the 80386 has other advantages in the way that it handles memory. For straightforward PC/MS-DOS applications it runs in the "real" mode (as does the 80286), and effectively just emulates the 8086. In the "protected virtual" mode (often just called

11

"protected" mode) it is much like the 80286 in its mode which gives a 16 megabyte memory address range. It has some extensions in this mode though, including a memory management unit (MMU) which provides sophisticated memory paging and program switching capabilities. Perhaps of more immediate importance to most users, the 80386 can switch from the protected mode back to the real mode much more simply and quickly than the 80286 can manage. A program running in real mode, but making use of extended memory and protected mode via a RAM disc or whatever, will therefore operate more quickly when accessing the extended memory. This is not purely of academic importance, and some methods of using the extended memory on an 80386 based AT are not worthwhile when implemented on an 80286 based AT as they simply do not work fast enough.

The 80386 has a third mode of operation called "virtual real" mode. The 80286 has no equivalent of this mode. In essence it permits the memory to be split into several sections, with each one running its own operating system and an applications program. Each program is run entirely separately from the others, and if one program should crash then all the others should remain running normally. Only the crashed section of memory needs to have its operating system rebooted and the program reloaded. This solves what has tended to be a big problem with many multi-tasking computers, where programs tend to crash regularly due to one program interfering with another, and with one program crashed the whole system tends to follow suit. The amount of memory that the 80386 can handle is so large (4 gigabytes, or some 4000 megabytes in other words) that even today's PCs can not actually take this much RAM.

There is a sort of cut-down version of the 80386, the 80386SX. This has a 16-bit bus like the 80286, but internally it has all the 80386 registers. This enables it to run 80386 specific software as well as standard PC software, albeit somewhat more slowly than on an 80386 based computer. The reduced speed is the result of the 32-bit pieces of data or instructions having to be loaded as two 16-bit chunks rather than being loaded simultaneously.

80386 based PCs are now well and truly out of date, and in most cases are probably not worth upgrading. There are exceptions though, and if a PC of this type has been kept up to date with new peripherals such as multi-media add-ons it might be worth upgrading to a modern specification. In order to do this it will still be necessary to renew much of the computer though (see chapter 6).

PS/2 Computers
When IBM ceased making the PC range of computers they were replaced with the PS/2 range. This should perhaps be considered as two ranges, since it consists of relatively simple machines that could reasonably be regarded as PC compatibles, and a more advanced range which are still basically PCs, but which depart from the previous standards in some quite radical ways.

The most basic of the PS/2 range were the Model 25 and the Model 30. These were 8MHz 8086 based computers which used standard ISA expansion slots of the 8-bit variety. They differed from earlier PCs in that they had a number of functions (such as the display generator circuitry) on the motherboard rather than requiring these functions to be provided by cards fitted in expansion slots. There was also a Model 30 286 computer, which was a 10MHz 80286 based computer having 16-bit ISA expansion slots. ISA (industry standard architecture) slots are the ordinary eight-bit and 16-bit PC expansion slots incidentally. The Model 25/30 and Model 30 286 computers were effectively more modern equivalents of the XT and AT computers, and PCs in the generally accepted sense of the term.

The Model 50, 60, 70, and 80 computers were more advanced computers which used a different form of expansion bus called "micro channel architecture", or just "MCA" as it is much better known. This is not really the place for a discussion of this expansion bus standard, since the subject of this book is the expansion of what for the want of a better term we will call

13

the traditional PC. The subject of MCA will therefore not be considered any further here.

80486

The 80486DX is essentially a more efficient version of the 80386 that requires fewer clock cycles per instruction, and has some extra instructions. It departed from the 80386 and previous processors in this series by having the maths-coprocessor built-in, rather than as a separate chip. The maths-coprocessor is a microprocessor that is designed to handle complex mathematics, and is mainly intended as a means of speeding up floating-point calculations. Virtually all PCs using an 80386 or earlier processor had a socket on the motherboard for a maths-coprocessor, but it was normally an optional extra and not fitted as standard. Most software did not require the coprocessor, and few PC users actually bothered to add one. The 80486DX encouraged software authors to make use of the maths-coprocessor, which it turned into a standard feature where it had previously been an expensive add-on. The 80486DX version of the coprocessor was more efficient than its predecessors, giving a useful increase in performance. There was a cut-down version of the 80486DX, the 80486SX, which lacked the built-in coprocessor. Like the earlier PC processors, the maths coprocessor was available as an optional extra.

The original 80486DX operated at a clock frequency of 33MHz, but some of the 80486SX chips were slower than this. Faster versions were developed over the years though, including some non-Intel alternatives to the 80486DX. I think I am right in stating that the fastest genuine Intel 80486DX operated at 100MHz, but non-Intel chips operating at up to about 133MHz were produced. The faster 80486DX based PCs are powerful computers, and if fitted with adequate RAM they can run a fair percentage of modern software. On the other hand, new software releases seem to place ever-higher demands on the hardware, and there is an increasing amount of software that will not operate on an 80486DX-based PC. There are processor upgrade kits that can be used to boost the performance of these PCs, and in many cases it is worthwhile spending money on a major upgrade to replace the processor, motherboard, and memory with modern components.

Pentiums

All modern PCs are based on an Intel Pentium processor, or a compatible processor from another manufacturer. Pentium processors have additional instructions, but are basically just faster and more efficient versions of the 80486DX. The original chips ran at 60MHz and 66MHz, and in most speed tests did not perform significantly better than the faster 80486 chips. Later versions used higher clock rates, fitted into a different socket, and had improved motherboards. This provided a boost in performance that gave much better results than any 80486DX PCs could achieve. The clock frequencies for these "classic" Pentium processors are 75, 90, 100, 120, 133, 150, 166, and 200MHz.

Although relatively recent, these processors are now obsolete and are not used in new PCs any more. Pentium processors with MMX (multimedia extension) technology replaced them. The MMX technology is actually an additional 57 processor instructions that are designed to speed up multimedia applications, but can also be used to good effect in other applications such as voice recognition. There were also some general improvements that produced an increase in performance by around 10 or 15 percent when using non-MMX specific software. These MMX Pentium processors were produced in 166MHz, 200MHz, and 233MHz versions.

These are now obsolete and have been replaced by Pentium II processors. At the time of writing this, Pentium II processors are available with clock frequencies of 233, 266, 300, 333, 350, and 400MHz, with 450MHz and even faster versions expected soon. The original Pentium processors fitted onto the motherboard via a conventional integrated circuit holder known as Socket 4. Those operating at 75MHz and above used an improved version called Socket 7. Pentium II processors look nothing like conventional processors, and in physical appearance they are like a cross between a videocassette and a memory module. They fit into a holder that is more like a PC expansion slot or holder for a memory module than an integrated circuit holder.

One reason for this change in style is that it potentially enables higher clock speeds to be utilized. Another reason for this change in style is that Pentium II chips are so complex that it is not possible to put the processor and cache memory on the same chip. Cache memory is high-speed memory that is used to store recently processed data. It is likely that this data will need to be accessed again, and having it available in high-speed memory ensures that it can be processed very efficiently when it is needed. In virtually all practical applications this significantly speeds up the rate at which data can be processed. Previous Pentium processors had some cache memory (typically 32K) on the chip, with a much larger cache of about 256 to 512K on the motherboard. These are known as level 1 and level 2 cache respectively. Level 1 cache is faster, but there are practical limits on the amount of cache memory that can be included in the processor. With the Pentium II chips it had to be omitted altogether, but a "piggy-back" memory chip included in the processor module provides a 512K cache.

The Pentium II is really a development of the Pentium Pro processor. This relatively unsuccessful processor was an improved version of the "classic" Pentium design, but when running Windows 95 software it often failed to provide much improvement over an ordinary Pentium chip. The Pentium Pro became overshadowed by the MMX Pentium processors, which proved to be an immediate hit with PC buyers. The Pentium II has the additional MMX instructions, and slightly improved performance compared to an ordinary MMX Pentium processor. The 350 and 400MHz versions are designed to operate on motherboards that operate at a 100MHz clock frequency and use fast memory modules. The slower Pentium processors operate with 66MHz motherboards and relatively slow RAM. This gives the 350 and 400MHz chips a greater speed advantage over the slower versions than a comparison of the clock frequencies would suggest.

Celeron

Intel has now abandoned Socket 7 technology in favour of the Slot 1 technology used for the Pentium II processors, and even higher tech Slot 2 processors are planned. The Intel processor for entry-level PCs is the Celeron, which is basically just a Pentium II with the add-on cache omitted. This saves on manufacturing costs, but clearly gives a reduction in performance. The Celeron has not exactly received universal praise from the reviewers, and the absence of any on-board cache gives it a tough time keeping up with the latest budget processors from other manufacturers. Its performance is actually quite respectable, being around 15 to 30 percent faster than an Intel 233MHz MMX Pentium chip, depending on the type of software being run. This is still well short of full 266MHz Pentium II performance though. At the time of writing this a 300MHz version of the Celeron has just been released, and a 333MHz version with 128K of on-chip cache should follow soon. Although the 128K is only one quarter of the cache fitted to a Pentium II, the fact that it is on the same chip as the processor (and therefore very fast) should to some extent make up for the smaller amount of cache.

Figure 1.1 summarises the Pentium chips produced so far by Intel.

Xeon

Neither the Xeon processor nor PCs that use it are available at the time of writing this, but they are both due out soon. It is a form of Pentium II processor, and initially it will be available in 400MHz and 450MHz versions. Some previous Pentium processors can be used in dual processor systems, which, with the right software support, gives significantly higher perform- ance than equivalent single processor systems. The Xeon takes things further, and can be used in four-processor systems, with eight-processor computers planned for the future. It uses Slot 2 technology, and is therefore physically and electrically incompatible with Slot 1 motherboards. With its larger and faster cache than earlier Pentium processors, together with a 100MHz

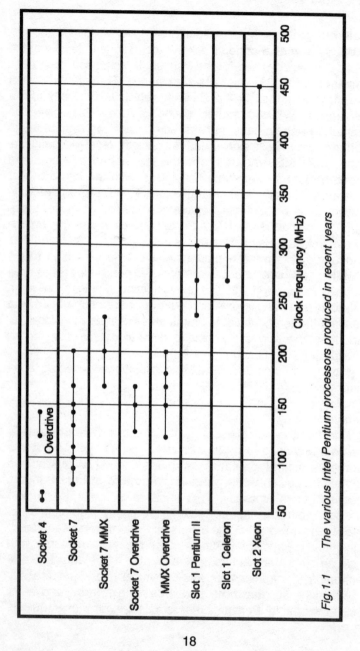

Fig. 1.1   The various Intel Pentium processors produced in recent years

18

system bus, this processor should be substantially faster than ordinary Pentium II chips.

Non-Intel

The manufacturers of compatible processors have, as yet, not shifted over to Slot 1 technology or their own version of Slot technology. They have instead opted to develop Socket 7 technology as far as possible. The front runners in compatible chips are AMD and IBM/Cyrix. The IBM/Cyrix chips are designed and developed by Cyrix, but manufactured by IBM. They are sold as both IBM and Cyrix processors. Here I will refer to them simply as Cyrix processors. Compatible processors are no longer on the fringes of the PC world, and they are used in a substantial proportion of new PCs, including some from "big name" manufacturers. So far they have proved to be capable of providing good performance and reliability at comparatively low cost.

The first AMD processor for PCs was the K5, which was produced in 75, 90, 133, 150, and 166MHz versions. This chip was an alternative to the "classic" Pentium processor. It was replaced by the K6, which has the MMX instructions, and clock frequencies of 166, 200, 233, 266, and 300MHz. This has now been joined by the K6-2, or K6-2 3D Now! to give this processor its full name. This is a Pentium style processor that includes the MMX instructions, but it also has its own set of instructions that, together with the later versions of Microsoft's Direct X system, enable 3-D games to run at increased speeds. This processor requires a motherboard that can operate at 100MHz and fast memory modules. It is intended to be a direct competitor to the Pentium II processors.

The Cyrix equivalent of the AMD K5 is the 6X86 processor. This was produced in 90, 120, 133, 150, 166, and 200MHz versions. These chips cause a certain amount of confusion, because their speed ratings are not their actual clock frequencies. For instance, a 200MHz 6X86 processor is a 200MHz chip in the sense that it offers performance that is broadly similar to an Intel 200MHz Pentium. The actual clock

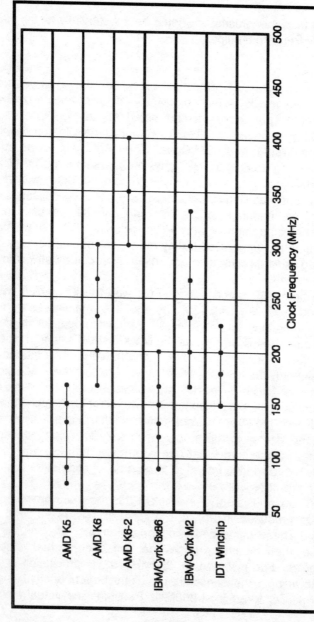

Fig.1.2   Chart showing the various non-Intel PC processors of recent years

20

frequency is somewhat less, and is actually 166MHz in this case. It has to be pointed out that how well (or otherwise) one make of processor compares to another depends on the type of software being run. Intel chips traditionally do well on floating point mathematics, but perform less well in other areas. If you are running a reasonably wide range of applications software, overall you are unlikely to notice much difference between equivalent chips from different manufacturers.

Cyrix produce processors that have the MMX instructions and these are the M2 series. These have clock frequencies of 166, 200, 233, 266, 300, and 333MHz. Like the 6X86 processors, the speed ratings of M2 chips are their equivalent clock frequencies, and the actual clock frequencies are lower (200MHz for the 233MHz chip for example). At the time of writing this, Cyrix has released nothing beyond the 333MHz M2.

IDT and its Winchip are relative newcomers to the world of PC processors. The Winchip is intended to be a low cost processor for entry level PCs. It has the MMX instructions, and is produced in 150, 180, 200, and 225MHz versions.

Figure 1.2 summarises the non-Intel Pentium class chips that have been produced so far.

System Make Up
A traditional PC is a so-called three-unit style computer. These three separate units are the keyboard, the main computer unit, and the monitor. They are connected together by cables, with a curly type normally being used for the keyboard. This is a convenient set-up in that it makes it easy to accommodate everything on practically any computer desk. Bear in mind though, that PCs are mostly quite large and heavy, and likely to prove both too big and too heavy for a low cost computer desk designed for a small home computer.

The main unit is comprised of several sub-units. The main ones are the case, power supply unit, motherboard, and one or more disc drives. Additionally, certain expansion cards must be present on the main board for the system to function. In the past it was necessary to have a hard/floppy disc controller card, plus a card or cards to provide standard interfaces such as serial and parallel ports. The current practice is for these functions to be provided by the motherboard, and the only essential expansion card is a video type to drive the monitor. In fact a few motherboards have an on-board display generator as well, but this is not a common feature. Although a sound card is not essential, a sound card and speakers has become a standard PC feature. The sound card usually includes a game port for joysticks, etc. This doubles as a MIDI port that enables the PC to be connected to synthesisers and other musical instruments or gadgets that have a MIDI port. A basic multimedia PC would consist of something like the following list of main parts.

Keyboard and mouse
Case
Motherboard fitted with BIOS and memory modules
14/15 inch colour monitor
SVGA display card with 2 megabytes of RAM
Floppy disc drive
Hard disc drive
CD-ROM
Sound card and speakers

A more up-market PC might have the following set of main components.

Keyboard and mouse
Case
Motherboard fitted with BIOS and memory modules
17/19 inch colour monitor
2-D/3-D display card with 8 megabytes of RAM
Floppy disc drives
Hard disc drive
CD-ROM drive
CD-ROM writer
Sound card and speakers
Modem for Internet connection

Some of these constituent parts, plus more specialised forms of expansion are discussed in later chapters, but there are a few aspects of these main parts that we will take the opportunity to discuss here.

Keyboards

The original PC keyboard was an 83-key type. At least, it was in its native (U.S.A.) form. The U.K. version had a slightly different layout plus an extra key in order to accommodate the pound sign (£), which was absent on the U.S.A. keyboard. The U.K. version was therefore generally known as the 84-key layout PC keyboard. This had ten function keys in two vertical rows of five, positioned to the left of the main QWERTY keys, and is now obsolete. 83/84 key keyboards were replaced by the enhanced layout that was introduced by IBM in 1986. This has 101 keys in its original U.S.A. version, or 102 keys in the case of the U.K. version. Twelve function keys on the enhanced layout replace the ten function keys of the original design. These keys are relocated to a single row above the main QWERTY keyboard (which is where the "Esc" key is also to be found). The numeric keypad/cursor key arrangement is retained, but only for those who are used to the original scheme of things and wish to go on using it. This keypad is moved over to the right in order to make room for a separate cursor cluster, etc.

The 102-key layout has now been replaced by the 105-key Windows 95/98 layout. This is basically the same as the 102-key layout, but there are three additional keys next to the spacebar. These bring up Windows 95/98 menus, and two of the keys have the same effect as operating the "Start" button on the Windows desktop. The third is equivalent to right "clicking" the mouse. As the additional keys are simply duplicating functions provided by the mouse, it is not essential to have a 105-key keyboard in order to use Windows 95/98. All current keyboards seem to have the 105-key layout.

If you look at the keyboards in a computer shop you can not miss the "ergonomic" variety, which have the two sides of the keyboard at different angles. They are designed to make touch-typing easier and less fatiguing, and seem to be liked by many touch-typists. Two-finger typists should stick to the traditional style PC keyboard.

The enhanced keyboards retain the original method of interfacing, and it is quite possible, for instance, to use a 105-key keyboard as a replacement for a 102-key, or even an old 84-key type type. This will not necessarily give perfect results though, since the BIOS in the computer may not be equipped to deal with a modern keyboard. Although most of the keys are merely duplicating those of the old 83/84-key layout, there are obviously a few additional ones that might have no effect when used with an old PC, or could produce the wrong characters. Any problems when using a new keyboard on an old PC are usually quite minor, and most users can live with them. Note that XT class PCs have the same type of keyboard connector as later PCs, but are nevertheless incompatible with modern PC keyboards. If the keyboard of an XT class PC fails, it must be replaced with a proper XT keyboard and not a modern one. The chances of finding a suitable replacement keyboard are quite small, since XT computers are now obsolete, and have been for some years.

A PC keyboard is a quite sophisticated piece of electronics in its own right, and is actually based on an 8048 single chip microprocessor (or "microcontroller" as these devices are alternatively known). This controller provides "debouncing", which prevents multiple characters being generated if the keyboard switches open and close something less than completely cleanly (which is always the case in practice). The keyboard controller also performs simple diagnostic tests, and can detect a key that is stuck in the "on" position for example. It also contains a 20-byte buffer, which is simply a small amount of memory that is used to store characters if one key is pressed before the character from the previous one has been read by the computer.

The keyboard also has multi-character rollover. In other words, if you press one key, and then another while still holding down the first one, the second key will be read correctly. In fact

24

you can hold down several keys and the next one that is operated will still be read correctly. I do not know how many keys can be pressed before this system breaks down, but attempts to overload the keyboard on my computers proved to be fruitless. Of course, like most computer keyboards and electric typewriters, the keyboard includes an auto-repeat function (i.e. holding down any character key results in that character being produced once initially, and then after a short delay it is repeated for as long as the key is pressed).

Connection to the computer is mostly via a five-way cable fitted with a 5-way 180-degree DIN plug. This is a form of serial interface, and the standard method of connection is shown in Figure 1.3. There is an alternative form of connector (the PS/2 type), which is a sort of miniature version of the standard type. This is becoming much more common, and when buying a replacement keyboard you must ensure that it has the right type of connector for your PC.

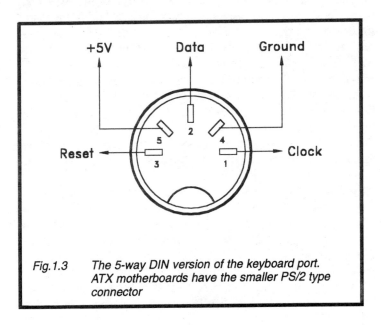

Fig.1.3   The 5-way DIN version of the keyboard port. ATX motherboards have the smaller PS/2 type connector

Motherboards

Unless you get into DIY PC assembly or repairs you may not need to know too much about motherboards, although background information of this type often proves to be invaluable from time to time. AT one time there were two main motherboard categories: the PC/PC XT type, and the AT type. However, the original XT and AT style motherboards are now well and truly obsolete, although modern motherboards are actually developments of the AT layout. I suppose that if you look at things in broad terms there are still two forms of motherboard, which are the AT and ATX varieties. The AT boards use what is basically the original AT layout, although modern AT boards are generally much smaller than the original design. Hence they are sometimes referred to as "baby AT" boards. ATX motherboards have a modified layout that puts the processor to one side of the expansion slots. Modern processors, when complete with heatsinks and cooling fans, tend to be quite tall and can obstruct several of the expansion slots. This prevents the slots from being used with the longer expansion cards. By moving the processor to one side this problem is avoided, and it is possible to use long expansion cards in any of the expansion slots.

There are other differences between the two types of board, such as the different power supply requirements and the on-board serial and parallel port connectors of ATX boards. The practical consequence of these is that the two types of board require different styles of power supply and case. When replacing a motherboard you must therefore be careful to replace it with one that has the same form factor.

AT and ATX boards can be further subdivided according to the processors that they support. When buying a replacement motherboard you must therefore make sure that it has the correct form factor and that it supports the processor you are using. Obtaining a motherboard to suit an early Pentium processor or any pre-Pentium processor can be difficult and expensive. Similarly, obtaining a replacement for an early Pentium processor or an 80X86 series processor can be time consuming and costly. If a fault occurs in the motherboard or processor of a PC that is something less than up-to-date it is often better to upgrade it to a more modern specification rather than try to do a straightforward repair job.

Chipsets
When looking at the specifications for Pentium based PCs and Pentium motherboards you will inevitably come across references to chipsets. These are the integrated circuits that provide various essential functions that are not included in the processor itself. In the original PCs these functions were provided by dozens of ordinary logic integrated circuits. Even though a modern PC requires much more help from the supporting electronics, there are normally just two support chips. Intel has manufactured various Pentium support chipsets, and these seem to be used on most motherboards. However, other manufacturers make support Pentium chips. Here are brief details of the Intel chipsets.

FX Early and basic Pentium chipset.

HX Early chipset that is in many ways basic but is also fast. Provides dual processor support. Used for both Socket 7 and early Slot 1 motherboards.

VX Early and basic chipset for Socket 7 motherboards giving SDRAM support.

TX Improved chipset for Socket 7 motherboards which provides support for SDRAM, USB, and UDMA33 hard disc interface.

LX First chipset specifically for Pentium II processors and Slot 1 motherboards. Provides dual processor, SDRAM, USB, UDMA33 and AGP support. Maximum memory of 512MB SDRAM, or 1GB EDO RAM.

BX Effectively an improved LX chipset that supports 100MHz

system bus and fast SDRAM. Up to 1GB or SDRAM or EDO RAM. Also supports 66MHz system bus for compatibility with 333MHz and slower Pentium II processors.

EX Optimised for Celeron processor. Up to 256MB of SDRAM or EDO RAM. No dual processor support.

GX Optimised for the Pentium II Xeon processors (i.e. 100MHz system bus processors) with no support for 66MHz bus.

NX Support for up to four Pentium II Xeon processors and 8GB of SDRAM or EDO RAM. No AGP support.

Configuration

For the computer to function properly it must know a few basic facts about itself, such as the type of display card and amount of memory fitted. This ensures that it produces an initial display properly, that it does not try to access memory it does not have, or ignore memory that it does have available. On the original PCs some switches on the motherboard were used for configuration purposes. AT class computers, from the originals to the latest super-fast PCs, have some low power CMOS memory that is powered from a battery when the main power source is switched off. This memory circuit is actually part of a built-in clock/calendar circuit, which the operating system uses to set its clock and calendar during the booting process. It is also used by applications software, such as a word processor when it automatically adds the date into a letter or other document. If a PC keeps failing to boot-up correctly, and takes you into the BIOS Setup program instead, it is likely that the back-up battery for the CMOS memory has failed. Most modern motherboards have a lithium battery that should last about five years or so. Older motherboards often have a rechargeable battery that is trickle-charged while the computer is switched on. If the PC is not used for a week or two the battery can run flat, but if the computer is reconfigured using the BIOS Setup program and left running for a few hours it should then boot-up properly again.

Configuring motherboards and using the BIOS Setup program is dealt with in the final two chapters of this book which deal with major PC upgrades and DIY PCs. Therefore, we will not consider this subject further here.

Maths Coprocessor
A maths co-processor is an integrated circuit, which looks very much like the main microprocessor in most cases. It is not normally fitted via an expansion card, but instead fits into a socket on the motherboard. Any PC processor from the full 80486DX onwards has the maths co-processor built-in, and not as an add-on chip. Therefore, provided you are using a reasonably modern PC it should be able to run any software that requires a maths coprocessor without having to resort to an upgrade. If you have an old PC that requires a maths coprocessor upgrade you are probably out of luck, because these chips are now obsolete.

Ports
While it is not inconceivable that a computer could be put to good use without the aid of printers, modems, and other peripheral devices, few people can utilize one in this way. Unless you are using a computer for an application where there will be no need to produce any hard copy, or transfer data via means other than swapping floppy discs, at least one parallel or serial port will be required. Modern PCs have two serial ports and a parallel port built-in, with the necessary hardware included on the motherboard. Connection to the outside world is via sockets mounted on the rear of the casing (most cases have holes for standard D type connectors ready cut), or mounted on expansion slot blanking plates. With ATX motherboards the connectors are mounted on the motherboard, and are accessed via cutouts in the rear of the case, rather like the keyboard connector of an AT style motherboard and case.

Probably for many users the serial and parallel ports supplied as standard with the PC will suffice. Most computers are connected to a printer, usually via a parallel port. This is the only parallel port peripheral used with many computer systems although parallel port scanners are now quite popular, as are various types of external add-on disc drive such as Zip drives. These all normally have a connector for a printer so that you can use one printer port to drive both a printer and a scanner or drive. If you should need an extra printer port, it is just a matter of adding a printer port card into one of the expansion slots. At present, parallel port cards invariably seem to be ordinary ISA types, and not the more modern PCI variety.

A mouse (or other pointing device such as a digitising tablet or tracker ball) is now a standard PC peripheral, and these can be of either the mouse port (PS/2) or serial varieties. There is also a third type known as a bus mouse, which is supplied complete with an expansion card that interfaces the mouse to the computer. However, the built-in mouse port of most modern PCs has led to the demise of this type of mouse. A serial mouse connects to a standard serial port, and on the face of it a mouse port mouse is the better option, as it leaves the serial port free for other purposes. In practice there is a slight risk of a mouse port mouse conflicting with other hardware, but it should be possible to sort out any hardware conflict that occurs.

Even with a printer and a serial mouse connected to the computer, the ports supplied as part of the standard system will almost certainly suffice. It is only if you need to add a second printer, a plotter, a modem, or some more exotic piece of equipment that further ports might be needed. You need to bear in mind that there is a limit to the number of serial and parallel ports that can be added to a PC. You can have up to three parallel ports ("LPT1" to "LPT3"), and up to four serial ports ("COM1" to "COM4"). Software supports for anything beyond LPT2 and COM2, used to be something less than universal. In fact some software, rather unhelpfully, seems reluctant to recognise anything beyond LPT1 and (possibly) COM1. Windows has eased this problem, and if Windows recognises a serial or parallel port it should be usable with any Windows applications software.

When buying parallel and serial port cards you need to

ensure that the card will provide the particular port you require. Most cards of this type now have configuration switches or jumper blocks so that they can be set to act as at least port 1 or port 2, and possibly as port 3 or 4. You may still some cards that have the port number or numbers preset. This is most common with single parallel and serial port cards, where the port is often preset as port 1. With twin serial port cards you sometimes find that the port is preset at port 1, with some optional components providing a second port that acts as port 2. However, with most modern serial and parallel port cards you have a large amount of control over the port numbering.

When expanding a system, you will almost certainly need a card to provide port 2 or beyond. Expansion cards that do not allow you to set the port number via configuration switches or jumper blocks are probably best avoided. Although you might be able to reconfigure one of the existing ports to operate as port 2, so that the new port can operate as port 1, these older boards often lack the capabilities of modern cards. For example, modern parallel ports have bi-directional modes that enable them to receive parallel data as well as send it. This capability is exploited by many modern peripherals that utilize a parallel port, including printers, scanners, and external disc drives of various types. Where possible it is preferable to leave the existing ports operating under their original numbers, and to have any new ports as port 2, port 3, or whatever. If you do need to reconfigure the built-in ports, it will be necessary to do so via the BIOS Setup program (refer to chapter 7).

When configuring serial and parallel ports you do not normally set them as LPT1, COM2, or whatever. Instead you set the port base address. In the case of a parallel port (and possibly a serial port) an interrupt number is specified as well. Port addressing works much like ordinary memory addressing, and it enables the processor to "talk" to the appropriate register in a selected piece of hardware. A hardware interrupt is where a peripheral device or a piece of built in hardware activates an input line of the processor to indicate that it has produced data that requires processing. Every time you move the mouse, for instance, it generates an interrupt. The processor then fetches and processes the new data, moves the cursor to the appropriate new screen position, and then carries on where it left off. This avoids having the processor waste large amounts of time repeatedly monitoring hardware devices that are idle.

This table shows the usual addresses and (where appropriate) interrupt numbers for COM1, to COM4, LPT1, and LPT2 (the addresses are in hexadecimal and are the base addresses. If a parallel port has a base address of 3BC (interrupt 7) it will probably be set as LPT1 by the operating system, and the other printer ports are moved one number higher.

PORT	ADDRESS	INTERRUPT
LPT1	378	IRQ7
LPT2	278	IRQ5
COM1	3F8	IRQ4
COM2	2F8	IRQ3
COM3	3E8	
COM4	2E8	

USB, Etc.

Although USB ports have been around for some time, and most modern motherboards include one or two USB ports, they have not been used a great deal in practice due to a lack of proper support from the Windows operating system. This has been rectified with the release of Windows 98, and USB seems likely to play an increasingly important role in the PC world. USB is a form of serial interface, but it is much faster than a conventional RS232C serial port. An ordinary PC serial port can, at best, operate up to about 115000 bits per second, whereas a USB port can operate at up to 12 million bits per second. In fact a USB port is potentially faster than a parallel port. Another advantage of a USB port is its ability to operate with more than one peripheral device.

Some scanners and other devices interface to the computer via a SCSI port (small computers systems interface and pronounced "scuzzy"), which is a form of high-speed bi-directional parallel port. A few motherboards have a built-in SCSI interface, but this is something of a rarity. There are numerous ISA and PCI expansion cards that provide SCSI ports, and many peripherals that require this type of interface are supplied complete with a suitable card and connecting cable (or they are offered as an optional extra). The card should be supplied with any necessary driver software to integrate it with the common operating systems. SCSI is sometimes used for high performance hard disc and CD-ROM drives, but with modern PCs having high speed UDMA33 hard disc interfaces built-in, it is probably not worth bothering with SCSI drives for a stand-alone PC.

There are other types of input and output port that can be fitted to a PC, such as analogue types. These are only needed for specialist applications such scientific and medical research. Being specialised items they do not operate under any true standards. Most hardware of this type is fitted into the part of the input/output map reserved for "prototype cards". The exact address range is sometimes adjustable so that more than one card of this type can be used in the computer. However, when purchasing this type of hardware you need to make detailed enquiries in order to ensure that it will fulfil your requirements. You need to be especially careful that it is compatible with any software you will wish to use with it, or that any information you need in order to exploit the interface with your own software is provided by the vendor.

Digitising Tablets
Digitising tablets are absolute pointing devices, rather than

relative types (like mice). In other words, whereas a mouse can only be used to indicate movement in a certain direction, a digitising tablet deals in definite screen positions. If you lift a mouse from its mat, move it to a new position, and then replace it on the mat, the on-screen pointer will not move. With a digitising tablet, if you raise the "pen" or puck from the tablet, and then move it, the on-screen pointer will not move. However, as soon as you lower the "pen" or puck down onto the tablet the pointer will immediately jump to the appropriate point on the screen.

Most software is no easier to use with a digitising tablet, and they then offer no real advantages. As they are several times more expensive than a mouse, this has led to them being far less popular. Where a program does properly support a digitising tablet, it might be well worthwhile paying the extra money for one. Some CAD programs only use part of the digitiser for controlling the on-screen pointer, with the rest being given over to menus that are used instead of on-screen menus. This leaves virtually the whole screen free to act as the drawing area. Usually the digitising tablet can accommodate a large number of menus, and user defined menus incorporating macros (a series of commands) can be used. This enables quite complex tasks to be performed with a minimum of effort, and is one of the most efficient ways of working.

A tablet is very useful for use with illustration programs, etc., where it is often necessary to trace existing artwork into the computer, and to do freehand drawing work. The ability of a tablet to operate using a "pen", or "stylus" as it is more correctly termed, makes it more suitable for applications where free-hand drawing is involved. Most people, even after gaining much experience with a mouse, find it difficult to use for freehand drawing. A stylus is much better for this type of thing, being very much like using an ordinary pen or pencil. Modern tablets are quite sophisticated, often using a lead-free stylus, and offering pressure sensitivity when used with suitable software. Pressure sensitivity is very useful when a tablet is used with software such as paint and photo-editing programs. The pressure of the stylus can be used to control line width, colour strength, etc., making it possible to accurately simulate real painting and drawing media. With the increasing use of PCs in graphics applications, digitising tablets are becoming more and more popular.

In the past there could be difficulties in using graphics tablets due to a lack of support in the applications programs. This problem has been eased to a large extent by the popularity of Windows 95/98. Any graphics tablet should be supplied complete with a Windows 95/98 driver, and with this installed it will operate as the pointing device for any Windows applications. Support for pressure sensitivity is not guaranteed, but this feature is supported by many Windows graphics applications. With most graphics tablets you can also have a mouse connected to the computer, and can move freely from one to the other. This is a useful feature, because some software is difficult to control using a tablet and stylus. Of course, you will need separate ports for the mouse and the tablet, but as most PCs have two serial ports and a mouse port this should not be a problem.

Soundcards

PCs have a built-in loudspeaker, but this is driven by some very basic hardware that is really intended to do nothing more than produce a few simple "beep" sounds. For anything more than this a proper sound card and a pair of active speakers is needed. Most soundcards do actually have built-in amplifiers, but they only provide low output powers and generally provide quite modest volume levels when used with passive speakers (i.e. speakers that do not have built-in amplifiers). The simplest soundcards only offer synthesised sounds, almost invariably produced using FM (frequency modulation) synthesis. This gives adequate sound quality for many purposes, but wavetable synthesis is better for music making. This method uses standard analogue synthesis techniques, but the basic sounds are short bursts of recorded instrument sounds rather than simple waveforms from oscillator circuits. This gives much more realistic results, although all wavetable sound cards seem to produce variable results. There are usually a few hundred different sounds available, and I suppose it is inevitable that some will sound more convincing than others. Modern soundcards can typically produce 32 or 64 different sounds at once, and they are capable of reproducing quite complex music sequences. Even the cheapest cards have the ability to record and play back in high quality stereo, and to play back pre-recorded sound samples (.WAV files).

Apart from three or four audio input and output sockets, soundcards normally have a 15-way connector that is a combined MIDI port and game port. When used as a game port it takes standard PC joysticks and similar devices. When used as a MIDI port it enables music programs to operate with MIDI synthesisers, keyboards, sound modules, etc. However, note that standard MIDI cables have 5-way (180 degree) DIN plugs at both ends, and are therefore incompatible with the 15-way D connector of a PC soundcard. A special MIDI cable is needed to connect a PC soundcard to MIDI devices.

PC soundcards are often equipped with an interface for a CD-ROM drive. The reason for this is simply that many people added a CD-ROM drive to their PC at the same time as they added a soundcard, since both of these items are required in order to run multimedia applications. Several CD-ROM interfaces have been used in the past, but only the ATAPI interface is currently used for low cost drives (the SCSI interface is used for some up-market CD-ROM drives). The ATAPI interface is the same as the IDE interface used for normal PC hard disc drives, and modern motherboards have two ports of this type, each of which is capable of supporting two drives. Any IDE port fitted on a soundcard is therefore of no value when the card is used in a reasonably modern PC, and if possible it should be switched off. Otherwise it is simply ignored.

Chapter 2

INCREASING MEMORY

With so many modern programs requiring large amounts of memory in order to work at their best (or to work at all in some cases), it is not surprising that adding memory is the most popular form of hardware upgrade. Memory upgrading is a potentially confusing subject, since there are now several types of memory in common use. PCs prior to the 80386 processor had their memory in the form of integrated circuits that plugged into rows of holders on the motherboard. In some cases there were about three dozen of these sockets. If you ran out of sockets it was possible to increase the RAM further using expansion cards, but this gave rather poor performance due to the relatively low operating speed of the ISA expansion bus. Memory expansion cards are now totally obsolete, but you can still obtain the chips for on-board memory upgrades. Memory in this form is quite expensive though, and upgrading an old PC is unlikely to be worth the expense involved. In this chapter we will only deal with memory upgrades to reasonably modern PCs that use some form of memory module.

Memory Map
Memory that comes within the normal 640K MS/DOS allocation is usually termed "base memory". If you have a reasonably modern PC there will be no need to expand the base memory, as the computer will have been supplied with the full 640K of RAM as standard. RAM, incidentally, stands for "random access memory", and is the form of memory used for storing application programs and data. The contents of the RAM in a PC are lost when the computer is switched off, and is, for all practical purposes, lost if the computer is reset (whether a hardware or software reset is used). ROM (read only memory) is used for programs that must not be lost when the computer is switched off, which in the case of a PC means its BIOS program. The

8088 series of microprocessors can address 1 megabyte (1024 kilobytes or 1024K) of memory, but in a PC only 640K of this is allocated to RAM for program and data storage. The rest is set aside for purposes such as the ROM BIOS and the video RAM. Figure 2.1 shows the memory map for a PC.

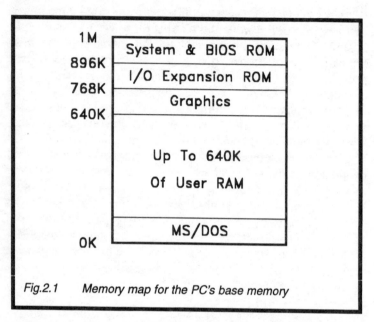

Fig.2.1   Memory map for the PC's base memory

Modern processors can operate in modes that permit large amounts of RAM to be accessed. Even on the most modern of PCs the maximum RAM limit is usually imposed by the motherboard design and not the processor, with an upper limit that is usually around 256 to 1024 megabytes. This is far more than is needed for most modern applications, the majority of which will run under Windows 95/98 with about 16 megabytes of RAM. This is not to say that these programs will not run better with more RAM. Probably the most frequently asked of frequently asked PC questions is "how much RAM do I need." This is very much a "how long is a piece of string" style question, and it is entirely dependent on the applications software that you will be running. The software manuals should give details of the minimum requirements, but the minimum is the bare minimum needed to run the software at all. Most programs can run in a relatively small amount of RAM by using the hard disc for temporary storage space. This usually works quite well, but gives noticeably slower results than when using RAM as the temporary data store. With complex graphics oriented programs the operating speed can be painfully slow unless the PC is equipped with large amounts of RAM. There will probably be a recommended minimum system to run the software, a typical system, or something of this type. I tend to regard the amount of RAM recommended for a typical system as the minimum that will really be usable in practice.

For most software at present, 32 megabytes of RAM is quite sufficient. A few applications require much more than this, and programs that handle photographic images or other large bitmaps are particularly demanding in this respect. When handling large bitmap images in PhotoShop for example, it is recommended that the amount of RAM in the PC should be at least double the size of the bitmap. In order to handle scanned bitmaps of around 25 to 30 megabytes at least 60 megabytes of RAM would therefore be required. Fitting the PC with 64 megabytes of RAM should therefore give workable results, but 96 or 128 megabytes would probably give noticeably quicker and smoother running. Bear in mind that large amounts of RAM can be needed in order to run several programs at once. In theory you do not need (say) 48 megabytes of RAM to multitask with two programs that require 16 and 32 megabytes of RAM. Somewhat less than 48 megabytes should suffice, because you are only running one copy of the operating system, and the two programs will share some resources. Practical experience would suggest that 48 megabytes would actually represent a realistic minimum in this situation.

Although memory has been very expensive in the past, it is currently quite cheap and putting large amounts of RAM into a PC is likely to be well worth the modest cost involved. Memory is like you know what and hard disc space: you can never have too much of it. You do not hear people claiming that they have wasted money putting too much memory in their computers, but you do hear people expressing regret for not having specified more RAM when buying their PC.

SIMMs

Until recently virtually all new PCs had their memory in the form of SIMMs (single in-line memory modules). A memory module of this type is a small printed circuit board, which is fitted with miniature DRAM chips of the surface-mount variety. This board plugs into a socket on the motherboard, and this set-up is like a sort of miniature version of the standard expansion slot system. 80386 and 80486 based PCs mostly use 30-pin SIMMs. These modules are available with normal eight-bit wide memory, and nine-bit wide memory. It is the nine-bit variety that is needed for most 80386 and 80486 PCs, but before buying any memory you should check this point in the manual for the computer or the motherboard. The additional bit, incidentally, is used for a method of error checking known as parity checking. These modules come in 256K, 1 megabyte, and 4 megabyte varieties, reflecting the type of DRAM chip they use. Only the 4-megabyte version is readily available now, but this is probably the only type you would require anyway. These modules are also available in a variety of speed ratings, again reflecting the type of DRAM chip they utilize. These days only the fastest (70ns) version seems to be readily available. With 80386 based PCs the modules normally have to be used in pairs or even in sets of four, but some 80486 can use odd numbers of these modules. There may also be restrictions on using SIMMs of different sizes. With many 80386 motherboards it is not permissible to use two 256K SIMMs in one pair of sockets and two 4 megabyte SIMMs in the other pair. Again, it is a matter of checking with the relevant instruction manual to determine what limitations apply to your PC.

There are some computers that have motherboards, which do not take either DRAM chips or SIMMs directly. Instead they have special plug-in memory cards, which in turn take either DRAMs and (or) SIMMs. I am not quite sure what advantages (if any) that this system brings, and it never caught on in a big way. This system has not been used on PCs built within the last few years. Note that the memory board slots on computers of this type are not standard memory expansion cards, but seem to be one-offs designed specifically for each computer. Unlike the old method of adding memory via ordinary expansion slots, no additional wait states are introduced when using these add-in memory cards, or when using SIMMs fitted directly onto the motherboard.

Bigger and Better
30-pin SIMMs are now obsolete, and have not been used in new computers for some years. They have been superseded by 72 pin SIMMs, which provide capacities of more than 4 megabytes per module. 72-pin SIMMs are available in 4, 8, 16, 32, and 64 megabyte versions. Like the 30-pin variety they are available with or without the parity bit. Unlike the 30-pin SIMMs, it is the modules that lack the parity bit that are normally used in PCs. Some motherboards can actually accommodate either type, but where you have the choice it is better to opt for the non-parity variety. These are significantly cheaper than the modules that have the parity bit.

Two types of memory are available in 72-pin SIMM form. The original modules of this type were fitted with fast page memory (FPM), which is basically just ordinary DRAM chips. More recently an alternative form of memory called extended data output (EDO) RAM became available. This usually gives somewhat faster performance than fast page memory, although the improvement obtained is unlikely to be more than about 10 percent or so. On the other hand, EDO memory no longer costs significantly more than the fast page variety, and is often significantly cheaper. It therefore makes sense to use EDO memory where possible, but it is not compatible with early Pentium motherboards, or any PCs of the pre-Pentium era. If in doubt, it is again a matter of checking the manual for the computer or the motherboard to determine which type or types of memory module are supported.

Although SIMMs are not exactly obsolete, they are steadily being replaced by DIMMs (dual in-line memory modules). These look like outsize SIMMs, and have 168 terminals. SIMMs operate from a 5 volt supply, but the DIMMs used in PCs operate from 3.3 volts (like the input/output terminals of a Pentium processor). However, 5 volt DIMMs are produced. Fast page and EDO DIMMs are available, but it is SDRAM (synchronous dynamic random access memory) DIMMs that are normally used in PCs. Many PC motherboards will actually operate with fast page and EDO DIMMs, but as these are more difficult to obtain, slower, and usually more expensive than SDRAM, there would seem to be no point in using them. Buffered and unbuffered SDRAM DIMMs are available, but it is the unbuffered variety that is normally required for use in PCs. SDRAM DIMMs are available with capacities of 16, 32, 64, and 128 megabytes, but many of the early Pentium motherboards that accept this type of memory are incompatible with the larger sizes. In fact some of the first boards to accept DIMMs will only take the 16-megabyte type.

Figure 2.2 illustrates the sizes of SIMMS and DIMMs.

SDRAM is available in various speeds. For ordinary Socket 7 and Pentium II computers the 12ns variety is sufficient, but the faster 10ns DIMMs are also suitable. PCs which use super-fast motherboards which operate at 100MHz, such as 350MHz and faster Pentium II systems, require 10ns SDRAM, but it seems that not all 10ns SDRAM DIMMs will work properly on these fast motherboards. They require memory modules that are usually referred to as "PC100" DIMMs in the advertisements.

There is a trend for motherboards to only have sockets for DIMMs, but there are plenty of boards that can take either type. A typical Socket 7 motherboard has sockets for two DIMMs and four 72-pin SIMMs. Some PC upgraders get into difficulty because they assume that it is possible to utilize all six sockets. Using a mixture of DIMMs and SIMMs is not a good idea, and is strictly prohibited with many motherboards. Even where the

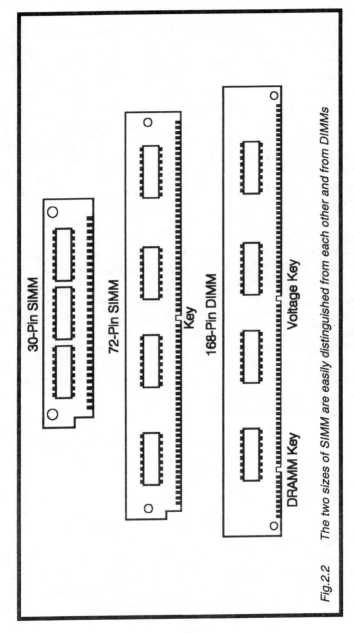

30-Pin SIMM

72-Pin SIMM

Key

168-Pin DIMM

DRAMM Key

Voltage Key

Fig.2.2   The two sizes of SIMM are easily distinguished from each other and from DIMMs

43

manufacturer of the motherboard does not ban this practice, I would certainly advise against it. The problem in using a mixture of the two memory types seems to stem from the fact that they operate at different supply voltages rather than any differences in their timing. Whatever the cause, I have never managed to get satisfactory results when using a mixture of these two types of memory module. If you read the "fine print" in the motherboard's manual you will almost certainly discover that one bank of SIMM sockets is connected to use the same address space as the DIMM sockets. Regardless of any other considerations, it is not possible to use both of these sets of sockets, as there would be a hardware conflict.

Right Memory

When purchasing memory for a modern PC it is clearly imperative to proceed carefully, as it would be very easy to buy the wrong type. There is really no alternative to reading the relevant section of the computer's manual, or the manual for the motherboard if that is what was supplied with the PC, to discover what type or types of memory module are usable. Do not use more than one type of memory. If the PC already has two fast page SIMMs, use two more fast page SIMMs to increase its memory and not a couple of EDO SIMMs. With very few exceptions, SIMMs must be used in pairs in Pentium PCs, but DIMMs can be used in multiples of one. It will sometimes be necessary to remove one or more of the existing memory modules in order to increase the memory capacity of the computer. With only a few memory sockets on the motherboard, you can not go on increasing the amount of memory fitted by simply adding more and more memory modules. It therefore pays to think ahead and fit large memory modules, rather than working your way up to high capacity modules, wasting a lot of smaller ones along the way.

If you are not sure of the way in which the memory of your PC is made up, one solution is to simply look inside to see which memory sockets are occupied. This may not be necessary, because the BIOS start-up routine usually produces a screen that gives this sort of information about the system hardware. The BIOS will probably report the amount of memory in each bank of sockets, and the type of RAM fitted. It is not possible to work out the best way of expanding the computer's memory unless you know what memory is already fitted. You really need to look at all the possible upgrade options, and cost them. Older types of memory tend to be more expensive than newer types, presumably because the older types of memory module no longer sell in large quantities. If your PC will take a more up-to-date form of memory than the type currently fitted, it might actually be cheaper to dump the original memory and start "from scratch". Apart from being cheaper, changing to a more modern form of memory will probably provide a modest increase in performance.

Fitting Memories
Fitting numerous RAM chips into their sockets is a tedious task, and it is easy to accidentally buckle one of the pins or fit a chip around the wrong way. Memory modules were produced in an attempt to make fitting and removing memory much easier, and something that practically anyone could undertake. Fitting DIMMs is certainly very easy, and it is impossible to fit them the wrong way round because the circuit board has a polarising "key". This is just an off-centre notch cut in the circuit board that matches a bar in the DIMM socket (see Figure 2.2). In fact there are two of these keys, and they are apparently in slightly different positions depending on the supply voltage of the module and the type of RAM fitted. This should make it impossible to fit a DIMM of the wrong type. Because one notch and bar are well off-centre it is easy to determine which way around the module should go. The module simply drops into place vertically and as it is pressed down into position the plastic lever at each end of the socket should start to close up. Pressing both levers into the vertical position should securely lock the module in place. To remove a DIMM, simply press the two levers outwards as far as they will go. This should unlock the memory module so that it can be lifted free of the socket.

In my opinion at any rate, SIMMs are slightly more awkward to fit. Although in theory it is impossible to fit a 72-pin SIMM the wrong way round, in practice it does happen occasionally. This seems to be due to the rather flimsy and slightly too basic SIMM holders used on some motherboards. There is the usual polarising notch in the module and matching bar in the socket, but they are small and only very slightly off-centre. Also, there is one corner of the circuit board missing. The old 30-pin SIMMs seem to be somewhat easier to deal with. They have the missing corner, but not the notch incidentally.

The method of fitting both types is exactly the same. When fitting SIMMs, orient the motherboard so that the sides of the sockets having the metal clips, are facing towards you, and the plain sides are facing away from you (Figure 2.3). Take the first SIMM and fit it into the first socket, which is the one that is furthest away from you, but it must be leaning toward you at about 45 degrees and not fully vertical. Once it is right down into the socket it should lock into place properly if it is raised to the vertical position. If it refuses to fit into position properly it is almost certainly the wrong way round. If you turn it through 180 degrees and try again it should fit into place correctly. You can then move on to the next socket, and fit the next SIMM in the same way.

Because SIMMs have to be inserted into their sockets at an angle, and the sockets are tightly grouped on the motherboard, you normally have to fit them in the right order. Otherwise you put in one SIMM which then blocks access to the socket for one of the others. You therefore have to work your way along the sockets in a methodical fashion. To remove a SIMM, pull the metal clips at each end of the socket outwards. The SIMM should then slump forwards at about 45 degrees, after which it is easily lifted clear of the holder. SIMMs have to be removed in the opposite order to the one in which they were fitted.

Memory modules are vulnerable to damage by static charges, and can be "zapped" by charges that are too small to produce any noticeable sparks and "cracking" sounds. They are normally supplied in some form of anti-static packing, which is

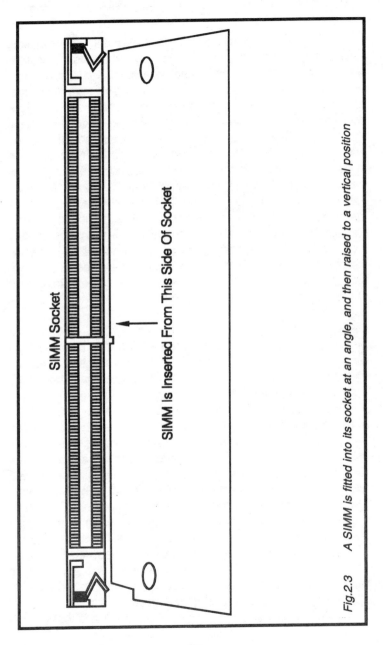

SIMM Socket

SIMM Is Inserted From This Side Of Socket

Fig.2.3   A SIMM is fitted into its socket at an angle, and then raised to a vertical position

most usually in the form of a bag made from conductive plastic. Always leave memory modules or any other static-sensitive components in the protective packing until it is time to fit them into the computer. You then need to make sure that both yourself and the memory modules are earthed, and therefore free from any static charges. The easiest way of doing this is to use the computer as an earth. It should be plugged into the mains supply, but must be switched off at the mains socket and at the computer's on/off switch. Even though the computer is switched off, its metal chassis will still be connected to the mains earth lead, which should ensure that it is reliably earthed. Before removing the modules from their packing, touch the metal chassis of the computer while holding the bag of modules. It is then safe to remove them from the packing and install them in the computer. You should obviously keep away from any known sources of static electricity when handling any vulnerable components.

Expanded Memory

The memory in a PC above the basic one-megabyte address range is called extended memory. There is an alternative method of obtaining memory above the basic one megabyte, and this type of memory is called "expanded" memory. It is often referred to as EMS (expanded memory system) or LIM (Lotus - Intel - Microsoft) memory. This second name is derived from the fact that these three large software houses got together to standardise this form of expanded memory. This type of memory was popular in the early days of PCs, because it can be used with XT class PCs that have an 8088 or 8086 processor. These processors can not address extended memory. The basic technique is to use a part of the address range in the upper 384K of the memory map. Although only a small block of addresses is available here, by switching between numerous chunks (pages) of memory it is possible to use this address range over and over again. Expanded memory is now obsolete, and is not required by any modern software.

Old Memories

If you need to obtain some memory for an old PC you will probably find that the speed rating of the memory modules is slower than that of the memory modules currently available. FPM memory modules usually have a speed rating of 60 or 70ns. Some early memory modules had speed ratings of 80 and 100ns. The speed ratings are sometimes marked on the memory modules themselves, but if not there should be a speed rating on the chips fitted to the modules. This rating is normally incorporated into the type number, and is usually at the end of this number. A chip marked "GM71C1000J70" is therefore a 70ns type, as indicated by the 70 at the end of the type number. The 1000 is its capacity in kilobytes, and it is therefore a 1MB 70ns chip. There should be no difficulty in using modern faster memory in an old PC, and there should be no problems if slow and fast RAM is mixed. Provided the entire RAM meets the minimum speed rating required for the motherboard and it is of the right type, there should be no problem. Trying to salvage old memory modules for use in a modern PC is likely to be less successful. Even if the old memory is of the right general type, the memory modules are likely to be of the wrong size (i.e. 30-pin instead of 72-pin). By using adapters it could probably be fitted into the newer PC, but would almost certainly to be too slow to operate reliably.

Chapter 3

DISC DRIVES

For a stand-alone PC at least one disc drive is an essential feature, because the operating system is loaded from a disc drive and is not built-in. While in theory a single floppy drive will suffice, these days the minimum requirement is a fairly large hard disc, one floppy drive, and a CD-ROM drive. Most software will actually run quite happily without a CD-ROM drive, but software is mainly distributed on CD-ROMs, and without a suitable drive there is no way of installing it onto the hard disc drive.

Floppy Drives
There are five types of floppy disc drive used with PCs, and these are listed below. All five types use both sides of the disc incidentally.

    3.5 inch, 80 track, 720K
    3.5 inch, 80 track, 1.44M capacity
    3.5 inch 2.88M capacity
    5.25 inch, 40 track, 360K capacity
    5.25 inch, 80 track, 1.2M capacity

The data on a floppy disc drive is stored magnetically on the metal oxide coating. This is much the same as the way in which an audio signal is recorded onto the tape in an ordinary compact cassette. In the case of a floppy disc though, the data is recorded onto a number of concentric tracks, or "cylinders" as they are sometimes termed. Each track is divided into a number of sectors, and there are nine sectors per track for a 5.25 inch 360K disc for example.

Originally the 5.25 inch 360K drives were used on PCs, PC XTs, and compatibles, while the 5.25 inch 1.2M type were used on ATs and compatibles. 3.5 inch drives have been adopted as the industry standard, and 3.5 inch 1.44M drives have gradually take over from the 5.25 inch variety. Even the 3.5 inch 720K type is now largely obsolete. 1.2M 5.25-inch drives are still available, although they are relatively difficult to track down. It is not uncommon for modern PCs to have a 1.44M 3.5 inch drive and a 5.25-inch 1.2M drive. The former is used to read and write new data discs, with the latter providing compatibility with the numerous 5.25-inch discs that many users (particularly business users) still possess. Of course, 5.25-inch discs can have their contents copied onto 3.5-inch discs, but this is time consuming and expensive if you have large numbers of old discs. Hence many users simply opt for the two-disc system, which will actually be required even if the decision to make 3.5-inch copies of old discs is eventually made. You need both sizes of drive in the same computer to carry out the copying.

The 2.88M disc drives were designed to replace the 1.44M drives as the standard for new PCs. With PCs tending to produce ever-larger files there is a definite advantage in the higher capacity of a 2.88M drive. Despite this, 2.88M drives have remained something of a rarity, and the vast majority of new computers are still fitted with 1.44M drives. The high initial price and a reputation for poor reliability certainly hindered the progress of the 2.88M drives. Consumer resistance to yet another change in the standard floppy disc format probably played its part as well.

Compatibility
Compatibility between the various formats is less of an issue than it once was, because many users now have only one size of disc and drive. However, you can still run into difficulty if you start dealing with old discs and (or) old PCs, so the following should be borne in mind if you have to deal with more than one disc format. Of course, 3.5-inch discs and the 5.25-inch varieties are totally incompatible, and you can only read a disc using a drive of the right size.

There is quite good compatibility between the two 5.25-inch disc formats. It is something less than perfect though. A 1.2M disc can not be read by a 360k drive, and it would be unreasonable to expect it to do so. Apart from the higher data density used by 1.2M drives, they also use twice as many tracks. With its wider record/playback head and only 40 head positions, a 360K drive will read two tracks at once when fed with a 1.2M format disc. A 1.2M drive can read 360K discs, and in my experience there are not usually any reliability problems when doing this. A 1.2M drive can produce 360K discs, but there is a potential problem if this is done. What the drive actually does is to miss out every other track, so that it only uses 40 tracks per side of the disc. This is not quite the same as a genuine 40-track disc, in that the 80-track drive is effectively using only about half the width of each of the 40 tracks. When read using a real 40-track drive this can, and often does, produce problems.

If you start with an unused disc, the half-tracks on which nothing is recorded will produce noise, but the disc drive may well be able to read the data through this increased noise. On the other hand, it might not! If the disc has ever been used in a real 40-track drive, and there has been data recorded across the full track width at some time, the chances of being able to read the data off the disc is negligible. The problem is that the original data on the disc is recorded across the full track width, but the 1.2M disc drive will only overwrite about half of each track. A 360K drive will therefore read back both sets of data simultaneously, giving a totally scrambled output. Paradoxically, another 1.2M drive will only read the half of the track which contains the wanted data, and will probably read a 360K disc of this type successfully, whereas a 360K drive will be unable to do so.

Compatibility between the two types of 3.5-inch disc is much better. The 720K drives can not read 1.44M discs, since they can not handle the higher data density. However, as both types of disc use 80 tracks, there are no problems if a 1.44M drive is used to produce 720K discs. They should be perfectly readable on both 1.44M and 720K drives.

Extra Drives
Most hard disc PCs are supplied with a single 3.5 inch 1.44M

floppy as standard, and for most purposes this is all that is required. However, if you will need to do a lot of disc copying it will be somewhat easier with the aid of a second floppy disc. As already explained, many users add a 1.2M 5.25-inch drive to provide compatibility with their old 5.25-inch discs.

The first point to bear in mind when adding a disc drive to a PC is that it must be of a type that is supported by the BIOS. Also, it must be a type that the computer's floppy disc controller can handle. There should be no difficulty when adding any standard size drive to a modern PC, since the BIOS and built-in floppy controller will support all five types. There can be difficulties when trying to add a modern drive to an old PC, because it is likely that the floppy disc controller and (or) the BIOS will not have support for a 1.44M or 2.88M drive. It might be possible to overcome such problems by obtaining a new BIOS or fitting a new floppy disc controller. In practice it could be difficult to obtain the necessary components, and very expensive even if they could be tracked down. Undertaking this type of upgrade is simply not cost effective.

There are two basic tasks to complete when fitting a floppy disc drive. The first is to get it physically fixed in place, and the second is to get it connected to the controller correctly. With modern PCs the disc drives normally fit directly into the drive bays, and are then fixed in place using two screws each side. These fit into the threaded holes in the side panels of the drives. If you are lucky, your computer will have been supplied with some additional drive fixing screws and one or two other odds and ends of hardware. Alternatively, disc drives are sometimes supplied complete with a set of four fixing screws. If not, it could be difficult to locate a source of suitable screws. It is important that these screws are quite short. Otherwise there is a risk of them penetrating too far into the drive and causing damage. Provided you have the correct fixing screws, fixing a drive into this type of computer is unlikely to give any real difficulties.

Old style AT cases use a somewhat different method of drive fixing. Two plastic guide rails are required, and these are bolted one per side onto the drive. The slightly pointed end of the rails should be towards the rear of the drive. This assembly is then slid into place in one of the drive bays, pushing it right back as far as it will go. With some cases a couple of metal clips are then bolted in place at the front of the bay. These press hard against the plastic mounting rails, and hold the drive assembly firmly in place. With most cases the drive assembly is bolted in place by two or four screws which go through holes in the drive bays and into threaded holes in the guide rails. If you look at the existing floppy disc drive you will see how everything fits into place.

The guide rails are almost totally standardised, but I have encountered one or two AT compatibles that seem to use a non-standard type of rail. If your computer falls into this category, and it was not supplied complete with an extra set of guide rails, adding an extra disc drive could be problematic. Possibly your dealer will be able to supply a set of suitable rails. Alternatively, you will have to improvise a bit with a standard set of rails, or make up some rails yourself from some scraps of plastic or wood. If your computer does use the standard type, it is quite likely that it will have been supplied together with an extra set.

Connections

You must also connect the power supply to the disc drive. Modern PC power supplies have about five or six leads and connectors for disc drives. Simply connect the plug on any spare lead to the power socket on the disc drive. This is a properly polarised plug, and it is impossible to connect it to the drive around the wrong way. With old PCs there may not be a spare disc drive power cable. You will then need to obtain an adapter which takes one of the drive power leads and splits it to permit connection to two drives. There is a potential problem in that there are two sizes of power connector. The larger type is used for 5.25-inch floppy drives, CD-ROM drives, and most hard disc drives. A miniature version of this power connector is used for 3.5-inch floppy drives. However, if a 3.5-inch drive is fitted in a chassis to permit it to fit into a 5.25-inch bay, this will probably include an adapter that enables the drive to be connected to a standard (full size) disc drive connector. Note that if you only have a spare 5.25-inch bay, and you wish to fit a 3.5-inch drive, you must obtain one of these mounting frames.

It is obviously a matter of looking at the drive and the spare power cables to see if a match can be found. If not, your local PC store should be able to supply a cable to permit a small power plug to be used with a standard size socket, or vice versa. Alternatively, one of the supply splitter cables mentioned earlier might provide a means of powering the new drive.

Floppy Cables

The standard PC floppy disc drive cable consists of a length of 34-way ribbon cable, which is fitted with 34-way edge connectors and IDC connectors at the floppy drive end. 3.5-inch floppy drives require the IDC connectors, and 5.25-inch types connect to the edge connectors. The connector at the controller end is not totally standardised, but any reasonably modern controller will require a 34-way IDC connector. Most cables are for twin drives, and therefore have two sets of drive connectors. This makes like easier when adding a second drive, because you can normally use the existing cable.

In a standard floppy drive set-up, the two connectors would be wired in exactly the same way. Pin 1 at the controller would connect to pin 1 of both drives, pin 2 would connect to both of the pin 2s, and so on. The two drives do not operate in unison, and both try to operate as drive A, because there are jumper leads on the drives which are set to make one operate as drive A, and the other as drive B. These jumper blocks are normally a set of four pairs of terminals marked something like "DS0", "DS1", "DS2", and "DS3" (or possibly something like "DS1" to "DS4"). The instruction manual for the disc drive (in the unlikely event of you being able to obtain it) will make it clear which of the many jumper blocks are the ones for drive selection. Drive A has the jumper lead on "DS0", while drive B has it on "DS1".

Things could actually be set up in this fashion in a PC, but it is not the standard way of doing things. Instead, both drives are set as drive B by having the jumper lead placed on "DS1". The so-called "twist" in the cable between the two drive connectors then reverses some of the connections to one drive, making it operate as drive B. This may seem to be an unusual way of doing things, but there is apparently a good reason for it. If you obtain a PC disc drive, whether for use as a replacement for a worn out drive A, or as a newly added drive B, the same drive configured in exactly the same way will do the job. This avoids the need for dealers to stock two different types of drive, which in reality is exactly the same type of drive with a slightly different configuration. For the DIY PC upgrader it makes life easier in that any drive sold for use in a PC should work perfectly without the need to alter any of the configuration jumpers. In fact many 3.5-inch drives are manufactured specifically for use in PCs, and do not actually have any configuration jumpers. Of course, if you buy a drive that is not specifically for use in a PC, it might not be set up correctly for operation in a PC. The elusive instruction booklet for the disc drive is then more than a little useful.

The computer will still work if you get the connections to two floppy drives swapped over, but the one you required as drive A: will be drive B:, and vice versa. The connector at the end of the cable couples to drive A, while the other one connects to drive B. Figure 3.1 shows this general scheme of things. When adding a drive to an older PC you might find that the cable only has edge connectors for the drives, but that the new drive requires an IDC connector. A suitable edge connector to IDC adapter could be impossible to obtain these days, and there will probably be no alternative to buying a new floppy drive cable.

Getting the floppy drive cable connected to the new drive should be straightforward, because the two connectors should be polarised, so that they can not be fitted the wrong way round. The necessary "key" is just a small metal rod on the edge connector, which fits into a slot in the connector on the drive. A lump and a slot on IDC connectors serve the same function. Unfortunately, the polarising "keys" are sometimes missing. You should find that the connector numbers, or some of them, are marked onto the connector on the disc drive and on the drive controller. Incidentally, on modern computers the floppy drive controller is usually part of the motherboard. They might also be

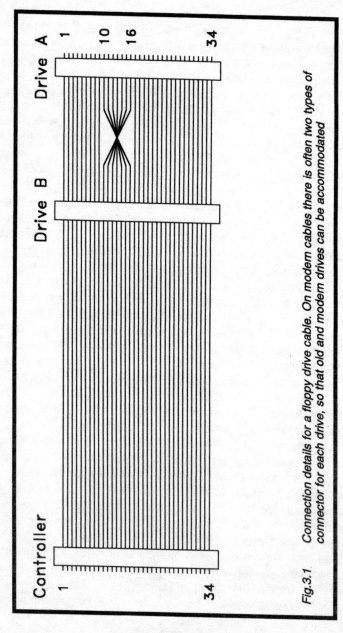

Fig.3.1. Connection details for a floppy drive cable. On modern cables there is often two types of connector for each drive, so that old and modern drives can be accommodated

marked on the drive lead connectors, and a coloured lead (as opposed to the grey of all the others) on the cable itself should denote the pin 1 end of the lead/connector. Pin 1 of the floppy drive controller couples to pin 1 of the drive's connector.

Termination Resistors

In the past every disc drive had a set of eight termination resistors. These connected to certain inputs of the drive, and tied them to the +5 volt supply rail. They are termed "pull-up" resistors. However many disc drives are used, only one set of termination resistors should be present. It is only the drive at the end of the cable that should have these resistors. Therefore, if you fit a second drive to a PC, as it will fit mid-cable, it will not require its termination resistors. These resistors are normally in the form of a single component, rather than eight individual resistors. They will be mounted in a socket of some kind, and this will often be of the standard 16-pin d.i.l. integrated circuit type. A socket of this type has two rows of eight terminals 0.3 inches apart. The resistor pack itself will probably be in the form of a black plastic component having two rows of eight pins. The resistors have a value of 220 ohms, and so the component will be marked something like "220R", plus some other characters in most cases. Some drives have a s.i.l. (single in-line) resistor pack. These have nine pins in a single row, usually with 0.1-inch pin spacing. Like the d.i.l. resistor packs, they are mounted in a socket so that they can be easily removed. In fact the s.i.l. variety are generally more easily removed than the d.i.l. type. With any d.i.l. component it is a good idea to use a screwdriver to carefully prise it free from the socket. Keep the termination resistor pack safe somewhere in case it should be needed at some later time. In fact you should always keep anything removed from the computer when performing upgrades. You never know when these odds and ends will be needed again.

It is only fair to point out that many modern floppy drives do not have removable termination resistors. With drives of this type you simply connect them up and hope they work (which they invariably seem to).

Hard Discs

A hard disc is very much like an ordinary floppy type, but in a highly refined form. The disc itself is a permanent part of the drive, and is not interchangeable like floppy discs (hence the alternative name of "fixed" disc). The disc is made of metal and is rigid (hence the "hard" disc name). The disc spins at a much higher rate that is about ten or more times faster than the rotation speed of a floppy disc. Furthermore, it rotates continuously, not just when data must be accessed. This is an important factor, since one of the main advantages of a hard disc is the speed with which data can be accessed. Having to wait for the disc to build up speed and settle down at the right speed would slow down disc accesses by an unacceptable degree. In fact the high rotation speed would result in accesses to a hard disc actually being slower than those to a floppy disc. A slight drawback of this continuous rotation is that computers equipped with hard discs are notoriously noisy! The high rotation speed of the disc aids rapid data transfers. Data can typically be read from disc in less than a tenth of the time that a floppy disc would take to handle the same amount of data. In fact modern hard drives are more like 100 times faster than floppy drives.

Although the disc of a hard disc drive is not changeable, it has a very high capacity so that it can accommodate large amounts of data and several large applications programs if necessary. This is achieved by having what is typically many hundreds of cylinders (tracks) with numerous sectors per cylinder. Early hard discs had capacities of about 10 to 20 megabytes, but the lowest capacity currently offered by most suppliers is in excess of one gigabyte (1000 megabytes). Hard discs having capacities of about four to eight gigabytes are quite commonplace. In most cases the "disc" is actually two, three, or four discs mounted one above the other on a common spindle. This enables around three to eight record/playback heads and sides of the disc to be used, giving higher capacities than could be handled using a single disc

An important point that has to be made right from the start is that hard discs are highly intricate and quite delicate pieces of equipment. Modern hard drives are somewhat tougher than the early units, most of which had warning notices stating that the mildest of jolts could damage the drive. Even so, they must be treated with due respect, and protected from excessive jolts and vibration if they are to provide long and trouble-free service. You are unlikely to damage a modern hard disc drive simply by picking up the computer in which it is fitted, and carrying it across to the other side of the room. On the other hand, dropping a hard drive or the computer in which it is fitted could well result in serious damage to the hard disc drive. Hard disc units are hermetically sealed so that dust can not enter. This is crucial, due to the high rotation speed of the disc. Apparently, the heads are aerodynamic types, which glide just above the surface of the disc, never actually coming into contact with it. If the two should come into contact, even via an intervening speck of dust, the result could easily be severe damage to the surface of the disc, and possibly to the head as well. Never open up a hard disc drive if you ever intend to use it again!

Interfaces

Adding a hard disc drive to a PC breaks down into three basic tasks. First it must be bolted in place inside the computer. Then it must be connected up to the power supply and a suitable hard disc controller. Finally, it must be formatted and made ready for use with the operating system. Usually the operating system will be installed on the hard disc so that the computer boots-up from the hard disc at switch-on. As we shall see shortly, formatting and making a hard disc ready for use is a slightly more complex business than formatting a floppy disc.

Physically installing a hard disc is much the same as installing a floppy disc. All PC floppy disc drives, with the possible exceptions of some very early types, are of the half height variety. The same is true for most hard disc drives, but some older and high capacity types are full height devices. In order to accommodate one of these you must have two spare drive bays, and they must be one above the other not side-by-side. You will also need two sets of fixing screws, slide rails, or whatever. As there is no disc swapping with a hard disc drive, it does not need to be mounted in a drive bay that has an open front. In fact the convention is for hard disc drives to be mounted out of sight in an internal drive bay.

A variety of hard disc controllers have been used in the past, but there are now only two types in common use. By far the most popular hard disc interface for PCs is the IDE type, which developed into the EIDE and UDMA33 hard drive interfaces. This is basically just interfacing the drive direct onto the ISA expansion bus, or in the case of the UDMA33 interface, onto the faster PCI expansion bus. The hard disc controller is contained within the drive. There is full compatibility between these three types of interface, and an old IDE drive should work perfectly well if it is connected to a modern UDMA33 interface. Similarly, a modern UDMA33 disc drive should work perfectly well if it is used as a replacement or upgrade drive in a computer that has an old IDE or EIDE hard disc interface. Of course, in order to gain the faster transfer rates of a UDMA33 drive it must be used in a PC that has a UDMA33 interface. Using an IDE or EIDE drive on a UDMA33 interface will not give an increase in performance either, but the drive will still work as a standard IDE or EIDE type. In order to get a UDMA33 drive to operate at full speed the PC must have a UDMA33 interface, suitable BIOS support, and an operating system equipped with a suitable hard disc driver.

With any reasonably recent PC there will be at least one, and probably two IDE ports on the motherboard. Connections from the controller to the hard disc drive are made via a 40-way ribbon cable, and most IDE cables have provision for two IDE devices. This is the maximum number that can be used with each IDE port, but with two ports on the motherboard up to four IDE devices can be accommodated. Most PCs only have a single hard disc drive, but the IDE ports can also be used for CD-ROM drives, CD writers, and high capacity drives that have removable media such as Zip and SparQ drives. It is therefore conceivable that all four IDE channels could be used, but two or three are usually sufficient. Unlike PC floppy drives, a twist in the cable is not used to determine which drive is the master IDE device and which is the slave type. Instead, configuration jumpers on the drives are used to set each IDE device as a master or a slave. There might only be the master and slave options, but there is often a third option that is called something like "cable select". This seems to be of no relevance in a PC context and should be ignored. With some IDE devices, but mainly hard disc drives, there are two master options. One of these is used where the drive is the only device connected to that IDE interface, and the other is used where there is a slave device as well. Before installing an IDE drive in the case you should read the instruction manual very carefully, and make quite sure that the unit is set up properly. The convention is for the boot drive to be the master device on the first IDE interface, although it will probably be possible to boot from the hard drive if it is used on one of other IDE channels. If you do not wish to boot from a hard drive it can certainly be used on any available IDE channel (as can CD-ROM drives and CD writers).

The IDC connectors used for IDE data cables are polarised, and in theory can not be connected the wrong way round. In practice the connectors on the motherboard are often simplified versions which allow the cable to be connected either way round. Also, the connectors on the cable sometimes lack the polarising "key" which ensures that they can not be connected the wrong way round. You then have to look carefully at the circuit boards, drives, and instruction manuals to find pin one on the IDE port and the drives. You then just follow the convention of making sure that the red lead of the cable connects to pin one of both the IDE port and drive connectors.

The only other common form of hard disc interface is the SCSI (small computer systems interface) type. This is actually a general-purpose interface that can be used wherever high-speed data transfers are required. It is not just used for internal devices such as hard discs and CD-ROM drives, and is often used with scanners and other external peripherals. Up to eight devices can be connected in chain fashion to a SCSI interface. SCSI hard disc drives have never been very popular amongst

PC users, and have mainly been used in network servers rather than stand-alone PCs. The speed advantage of SCSI hard discs has been largely eroded by the UDMA33 interface, and the substantial additional cost does not seem to be justified for most stand-alone PCs.

Formatting
Once you have configured the jumpers on the hard drive, mounted it in the case, and connected it to the controller and the power supply, it is time to switch on and try it out. However, there is still a fair amount of work to do before the computer will boot from the hard drive. The first step is to go into the BIOS Setup program and enter the appropriate parameters for the particular drive you are using. The BIOS Setup program is covered in detail in chapter 7, so refer to this chapter if you unsure about configuring the BIOS to operate with a new hard disc. Note that it is also necessary to change the BIOS configuration if a floppy disc drive is added. When using a high capacity drive in an old PC there can be problems due to the BIOS not supporting disc capacities of more than 528 megabytes. This does not mean that a hard disc having a capacity of more than 528 megabytes is unusable with a computer of this type, but it does mean that it can only use the first 528 megabytes of its capacity. If you set drive parameters that give a higher capacity the BIOS will not accept them.

There are actually ways around the 528-megabyte limit, and some hard drives are provided with utility software that can handle this problem. However, there is no guarantee that this type of quick fix will not produce problems in use. Fitting a more modern BIOS or (where possible) upgrading the program in the existing BIOS ROMs is a better solution, but is often impractical. Finding a more modern BIOS that is compatible with the motherboard is likely to be problematic, and could also be quite costly. It would probably be more cost effective to undertake a major upgrade, including the replacement of the motherboard with a modern type having a BIOS that properly supports modern high capacity drives.

Once the BIOS has been dealt with it should be possible to boot from an MS-DOS or Windows 95/98 system disc in floppy drive A. If the computer is otherwise working but will not boot from drive A, it is probably because it has not been configured to attempt to boot from drive A. This can be corrected by going back into the BIOS Setup program and setting a suitable boot-up sequence, which means any sequence that includes drive A. In the BIOS Setup program you will probably find a section that can undertake a low-level format of the hard disc drive. Unlike a floppy drive, a hard disc must be low level formatted before it can accept high level formatting from the operating system. However, IDE hard drives are supplied with the low level formatting already done, and a low-level formatting program must not be used to process them.

With the computer booted-up and running MS-DOS or the Windows 95/98 equivalent of MS-DOS, the hard drive will not be accessible. It must be high-level formatted using the MS-DOS "FORMAT" program, but first you must first prepare the disc using the "FDISK" command. The system disc in drive A should contain copies of both programs, and it is also helpful if this disc contains a simple text editor program such as the MS-DOS EDIT program. FDISK is used to create one or more DOS partitions, and with discs of 2.1 gigabytes or less you may wish to have the whole of the disc as a single partition. The hard disc drive then becomes drive C. By creating further partitions it can also operate as drive D, drive E, etc. Note that if you only require a single partition you must still use the FDISK program to set up this partition, and that the FORMAT program will not work on the hard drive until FDISK has created a DOS partition.

If two partitions are used, the primary partition of the hard disc will act as drive C, with the second partition operating as drive D. Some hard discs are supplied complete with partitioning software that will also format the disc and add the system files, which will be copied from the boot disc. Where a utility program of this type is available it is probably better to use it instead of the FDISK and FORMAT programs. These MS-DOS programs are fairly straightforward in use, but the software supplied with the drive will almost certainly be even easier to use. If you use the FDISK and FORMAT programs, make sure that you are using modern versions of them. Versions of MS/DOS earlier than version 3.3 are not able to provide two partitions.

Having followed the prompts and completed the "FDISK" command (simply accepting the default options is all that is needed in most cases), the "FORMAT" command can then be run. Due to the high disc capacity it take several minutes to complete the task, since there are a large number of tracks to be processed and checked. Presumably the operating system will need to be placed onto the disc, and this can be accomplished during the high level formatting process by including the "/S" parameter in the format instruction (i.e. "FORMAT C\: /S (RETURN)"). Alternatively, it can be added afterwards using SYS.COM. If the disc is operating as drive C, drive D, etc., each partition must formatted using a separate "FORMAT" command. Of course, the system should only be placed on disc C.

Operating System
If you are still using MS-DOS, the PC is more or less ready to use once the hard drive is bootable. You will have to install all your applications software or course, and it is a good idea to copy the MS-DOS support files to a directory call "DOS", or something similar. Windows 3.1 can be installed onto the hard disc in much the same way as applications programs. For most users, putting the MS-DOS operating system onto the hard disc is simply a stepping-stone to installing Windows 95/98. In the unlikely event that you have the floppy disc version of Windows 95/98 there should be no difficulty in loading it onto the hard disc once the hard disc is bootable. You may find that you need to install the mouse in MS-DOS first, but otherwise it can be installed onto the bare drive. The situation is similar with the CD-ROM version, but it is necessary to install the mouse and the CD-ROM drive into MS-DOS before the Windows Setup program can be run. This is simply because MS-DOS will not automatically recognise the CD-ROM drive and designate it as

drive D, or whatever. Just the opposite in fact, and MS-DOS will totally ignore the CD-ROM drive until the installation process has been completed and the computer has been rebooted.

The mouse and the CD-ROM drive should be supplied complete with installation software that largely does the installation for you. Some CD-ROM manufacturers supply the MS-DOS MSCDEX.EXE file, which is needed to integrate the CD-ROM drive with MS-DOS, but in most cases you will have to ensure that it is already on the hard disc. This file is supplied as part of MS-DOS 5 and 6, and should be placed on the hard disc if you install all the MS-DOS support files. It is installed into the C\:\\Windows\\Command directory once Windows 95/98 is installed, but this is obviously of no use at this stage, as Windows is not yet installed on the PC. If necessary, "borrow" this file from another PC by copying it onto a floppy disc, and then copying it to the hard disc drive. Alternatively, if you have a Windows 98 "recovery disc", boot-up from this and choose CD-ROM support when asked to select the start-up mode. This should provide access to the CD-ROM drive so that the Windows installation disc can be run.

Once the mouse and CD-ROM drive have been installed it should be possible to run the Setup program on the Windows 95/98 installation disc, and it is then just a matter of following the on-screen prompts to complete the Windows installation. Note that you can install the upgrade version of Windows 95 or 98 onto a "clean" hard disc, and that it is not essential to load your old version of Windows first so that you have something to upgrade. However, during the installation process you will probably be asked to prove that you have a qualifying upgrade product by putting the Setup disc into the floppy drive or CD-ROM drive, as appropriate. Do not throw away or recycle your old Windows discs, as this could leave you unable to reinstall the Windows upgrade

When upgrading to a larger hard disc drive you will no doubt have applications plus configuration and data files that you would like to transfer to the new drive. One way of achieving this is to use a commercial utility program to copy everything from the old drive to the new drive. With the right utility you can even copy the system files across to the new drive in such a way that it will boot up and behave exactly like the original. This can obviously save a great deal of time, but it not the method that I use. Windows tends to become cluttered with files that no longer serve any useful purpose, and reinstalling everything onto the new drive "from scratch" effectively removes any of the left-over files. Copying an exact image of a hard drive copies all the unwanted files as well as those that are really needed. Having reinstalled all your applications you can then copy data and configuration files across from the old drive. Obviously the old drive will have to be installed in the computer while the copying is carried out. It will be necessary to fit it into the case properly if you are going to leave the old drive in place and use it alongside the new one. Obviously this will only be possible if the case has sufficient drive bays to accommodate it. Most modern cases are unlikely to be "caught short", but with older desktop and mini tower cases you could be out of luck. If the old drive will only be needed while the files are transferred, it can simply be placed on top of the drive bays on a piece of card. The card will ensure that any connections on the underside of the drive do not short circuit to the metal case.

The Rest
There are now numerous other types of internal drive for PCs, including CD-ROMs, CD-ROM writers, and various types of removable hard disc drive. Installing one of these is very much like installing a hard disc drive, and the new drive will normally interface to one of the IDE ports. There are a few exceptions, such as drives, which use a SCSI interface card, or their own dedicated interface card. With IDE drives it is a matter of going into the BIOS Setup program to see if there is specific support for the type of drive you are fitting. There are often options for CD-ROM, Zip, and LS120 drives, but you are unlikely to find specific settings for any other drives. The drive's instruction manual should give advice on this aspect of things, but in most cases it is just a matter of setting the appropriate IDE channel

as occupied, but with all the parameters set to zero. The drive should be supplied with drivers for the popular operating systems, together with full installation instructions.

When buying removable hard disc drives, CD ROM writers, etc., you need to make sure you know exactly what you are buying, and that it is suitable for use in your system. IDE versions of some drives are only usable if they are supported by the BIOS in your PC. If not, either an external parallel port or SCSI version of the drive will have to be used. If the drive requires a SCSI or other form of controller card, is it supplied as standard or is it an optional extra? A suitable controller card can be quite expensive, and in some cases it costs nearly as much as the bare drive it controls. With a CD-ROM writer or CD-RW drive, is it supplied with full supporting software? These drives can be used in Windows 95/98 much like any other drive, albeit with some restrictions. However, they can only do so with the aid of suitable software, such as Adaptec's Easy CD Creator. Again, this type of software can significantly add to the cost of a drive if has to be bought as an extra.

Chapter 4

DISPLAYS, MODEMS, ETC.

I suppose that one of the greatest strengths of the PC family is its wide range of display types. Whereas most other microcomputers have the display circuit included on the main board, with no easy way (and possibly no way at all) of using an improved display, on the PCs the display circuit is on a standard expansion card. With built-in display circuits there is an understandable tendency for the designer to compromise between the number of graphics colours and resolution on the one hand, and cost on the other. This has often led to a display that is capable of reasonable colour graphics, but one which is not outstanding in this respect. A display of this type may seem to be a good compromise, but it limits the usefulness of the computer, and makes it virtually unusable in some demanding graphics applications.

In the past, if all you wanted was a PC having a simple text display or relatively low-resolution graphics, then there were low cost display boards to suit your needs. If you needed something a bit more exotic, there were high-resolution colour and monochrome graphics boards available. At the top end of the market there were various "power" graphics boards, which included on-board "intelligence" that enabled them to produce very high-resolution multi-colour graphics, but still operate at very fast speeds. Things have moved on, and the most simple of PC graphics cards now offer multi-coloured high-resolution graphics, and a certain amount of built-in "intelligence" to speed up graphics performance. While a display card of this type and a matching monitor are slightly "over the top" if you will do nothing more than basic word processing, their cost is likely to be much less than a basic monochrome text display of ten or twenty years ago. There are up-market video boards that provide super-fast, ultra-high resolution, true-colour graphics if that is what you need, together with large monitors that will do

71

them justice. There are also video cards that have built-in processing to provide fast 3-D graphics. These are mainly aimed at home users who require the ultimate in performance from the latest action games.

Resolution and Colours

There were several standard display boards for the early PCs, but anything up to the EGA (enhanced graphics adapter) graphics card now has to be regarded as completely obsolete. Modern display cards are compatible with the VGA (video graphics array) and its 640 by 480 pixel mode, which offered 16 colours. This mode is really just included as a sort of basic mode that is common to all video cards, and it is only required when installing the Windows 95 or 98 operating system, or when things go wrong. If the computer will not boot Windows 95/98 properly, trying to boot in "safe mode" will normally get the computer up and running so that diagnostic checks can be carried out. However, it will only work in a very simple fashion, including the basic 640 by 480 pixel 16-colour VGA screen mode.

Once Windows has been installed it is normal to go to the Control Panel, double-click on the Display icon, and then choose "Settings" so that the required screen mode can be selected. The range of screen modes available depends on the particular video card and monitor you are using. It also depends on the amount of memory fitted to the video card. The picture displayed on the monitor is made up of a matrix of tiny dots, or pixels as they are called. By setting the right dots to the right colours the monitor can display text, line graphics, or even photographic colour images. The picture is controlled by some memory on the video card, and the higher the resolution of the display, the greater the amount of memory that is needed to store the picture. Also, the greater the number of colours that the display can handle, the greater the amount of memory needed to store the picture.

With a maximum of 16 colours each byte of memory can handle two pixels. A basic 640 by 480 screen operating in 16 colours therefore requires about 150K or so of memory, because there are just over 300000 pixels. Modern video cards normally have at least two megabytes of video memory as standard, and boards with four, eight, or even 16 megabytes of video memory are now quite commonplace. This permits very high resolutions to be achieved, complete with huge numbers of colours, but only if the computer is equipped with a monitor that can handle these high resolutions. This table shows the number of bytes required for the colour depths normally used with PCs.

Colour Depth	Bytes Required
16	0.5
256 (8-bit)	1
65536 (16-bit)	2
16.7 million (24-bit)	3

Displays that can handle 24 bits or thereabouts are sometimes called "true-colour" displays, because they can handle more colours than the human eye can perceive. Of course, in reality the output device, be it a monitor or a printer, will place some restrictions on the available colours. Despite advances in modern technology, every output device still has some colours that are beyond its capabilities. On the other hand, with a 24-bit display card and a good monitor some quite stunning photographic images can be produced. Even some of the cheaper colour printers can now produce some excellent results that rival photographic prints, and this is an area in which computer systems have advanced enormously in recent years.

In general, the higher the resolution of the display the better it will be to use. The importance of colour-depth really depends on the type of applications being run. A 256-colour display is more than sufficient for something like basic technical drawing using a CAD (computer aided design) program or for straightforward word processing. 16-bit colour ("High-Colour") is adequate for complex colour graphics and colour photographs, but 24-bit operation gives significantly better results. With two megabytes of video RAM a basic video adapter can handle a wide range of standard video modes. This table lists the most common resolutions supported by PC video cards and monitors, together with the approximate amount of RAM required for 8-bit, 16-bit, and 24-bit operation.

Resolution	8-Bit	16-Bit	24-Bit
640 x 480 (VGA)	307K	614K	921K
800 x 600 (SVGA)	480K	960K	1.44M
1024 x 768 (XGA)	786K	1.57M	2.36M
1152 x 864	995K	1.99M	2.98M
1280 x 1024	1.31M	2.62M	3.93M
1600 x 1200	1.92M	3.84M	5.76M

Note that this table gives the approximate amount of video RAM needed for a standard 2-D display. 3-D displays require substantially more RAM, and typically require about twice as much video RAM at any screen resolution and colour-depth.

When reading the advertisements you will often come across references to types of video RAM, such as SDRAM, WRAM, and SGRAM. These are all forms of high speed RAM that are designed to give improved graphics performance. While some forms of video RAM are faster than others, fast RAM and top of the range graphics performance are not necessarily the same thing. You need to judge video cards by their overall performance and not by the type of video RAM fitted. You will also see references to the speed of the DAC (digital to analogue converter) or RAMDAC in advertisements and specification sheets. The monitors used with PCs require analogue signals to control the colours displayed and their luminosity. They can handle an infinite variety of colours within their colour range. Video cards deal in digital signals, which must be converted to corresponding analogue voltages by the card's digital to analogue converter. The faster the converter, the better the card is able to handle modes that involve high resolution and lots of colours. A fast converter does not necessarily mean perfect pictures at high resolution though. There are many other factors that govern the final display quality.

All Change
If you have an old PC it can be difficult or impossible to upgrade the video card. The problem is simply that older PCs only have ISA expansion slots, whereas modern video cards are for PCI expansion slots, or the more recent (and potentially faster) AGP slots. Finding a replacement video card for an ISA slot can be difficult, and no modern ISA video cards are produced. The situation is similar with VESA video cards. The VESA expansion slot was a rival to the PCI type for a while, but the VESA standard lost the battle and is now obsolete. VESA versions of modern video cards are not produced, and obtaining replacement VESA video cards is likely to be problematic.

If you are not sure whether your computer has ISA, PCI, VESA local bus, or some mixture of these expansion slots, the instruction manual should give the necessary details. Alternatively, open up the computer and look at the motherboard. If all the expansion slots are of the same type, only ISA expansion slots are fitted. A VESA slot is similar, but has an additional connector in front of the ordinary ISA type. Due to its large size and multiple connectors you can not mistake a VESA slot for any other type. PCI slots are much smaller, and the connectors on the motherboard are usually coloured white so that there is no risk of them being mistaken for the eight-bit ISA slots. Only modern motherboards have an AGP slot. This type is smaller than any of the other expansion slots, and is set further forward. Figure 4.1 should help in identifying the different types of slot.

Modern video cards only achieve top performance when used with powerful processors, so even if it was possible to fit a modern video board into an old PC it would probably give relatively little improvement in video performance. This is something that should be borne in mind when upgrading a 80486 PC that does have some PCI expansion slots. In order to

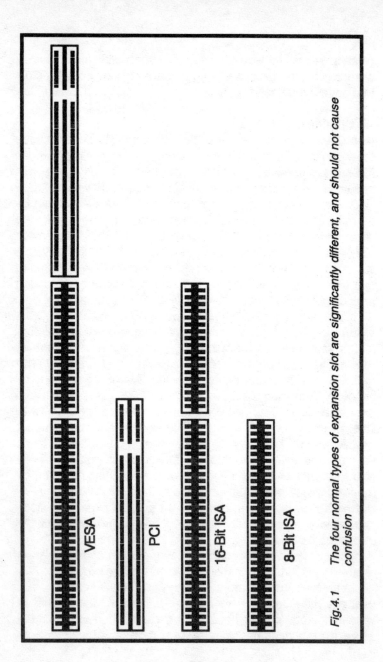

VESA

PCI

16-Bit ISA

8-Bit ISA

Fig.4.1   The four normal types of expansion slot are significantly different, and should not cause confusion

obtain super-fast graphics from an old PC it is normally necessary to undertake a major upgrade involving the replacement of the video card, motherboard, processor, and memory. This subject is given detailed coverage in chapter 6.

Assuming you can find a modern video card that is compatible with your PC, the hardware upgrade involves nothing more than disconnecting the monitor from the PC, opening up the PC and removing the old card, replacing it with the new one, reassembling the case, and reconnecting the monitor. Video cards, like virtually all complex PC expansion cards, are vulnerable to static charges. Touch the metal chassis of the computer to earth yourself before removing the card from its inner packing. It is then a matter of getting Windows to recognise the new card and use it properly. With Windows 3.1 it is best to set the PC to operate in a standard VGA mode before you fit the new card. To do this, run the Windows Setup program from MS-DOS and select the appropriate options. The Setup program will be found in the Windows directory, but there will probably be a PATH command installed during boot-up that will enable it to be run from the root directory. With the new video card fitted and the computer switched on, Windows should run properly, but only in standard VGA mode. The drivers for the new card must then be installed manually. Once the required video mode has been selected, Windows should operate in this higher resolution multi-colour mode.

With Windows 95 or 98 there should be no need to change the video mode before fitting the new card. During boot-up the operating system should detect the new hardware, and you then follow the on-screen instructions to install the drivers. If the "plug-n-play" feature should fail to work properly, you will probably have to re-boot the computer, and press the F8 function key when Windows starts to load, so that the operating system starts in "safe mode". In fact the computer will probably insist on starting in "safe mode" anyway. It is then a matter of going to the Control Panel, selecting "Add/Remove Hardware", and then installing the video card manually. There is the option of letting the computer automatically detect the new hardware, so you can give the automatic detection process a second chance if you wish. The fully manual approach is probably the better bet though. Once the new video card is fully installed, you can set the required mode by going to the Control Panel, double clicking on the display icon, and then selecting Settings.

It is common practice for modern video cards to be offered with various amounts of RAM. Typically a 2-D/3-D board would be offered in two, four, and eight-megabyte versions. In most cases, but not all, it is possible to add more RAM later, and there will then be a socket or sockets on the board to accommodate this memory. The type of memory used and its physical form varies from card to card. It might require standard memory chips, chips specific to the card, or memory modules that may or may not be a standard type. If you are contemplating a video memory upgrade it is first a matter of reading the card's instruction manual carefully to determine what is and is not possible. Then contact your computer component supplier to see if they have the right type of memory. Make sure you state that the memory is needed as an upgrade for a video card, and that you state the exact make and model of card you are using. If the memory then turns out to be unsuitable you are entitled to return it for a refund. If you simply order the wrong thing you will probably be charged a "restocking" fee if you return it, and the retailer may not be prepared to take it back at all.

A few of the more recent motherboards have a video adapter built-in, and in some cases there is an on-board sound generator as well. This harks back to the early days of computers when it was the norm for home computers to have the sound and video generators on the main board. If you do not require the ultimate in video or sound performance these on-board generators are very cost effective. On the other hand, you do not get "something for nothing" in the computer world, and if four megabytes of the computer's RAM is given over to the video circuits, there are four megabytes of memory less for the operating system and applications programs. Similarly, if the sound card uses a megabyte or two of the system RAM for storing sound samples for wavetable synthesis, there will be that much RAM left for other purposes.

Monitors

Having chosen a graphics card, you need to check that the monitor you have will match it properly, and support the display modes that you will require. Assuming that the existing monitor at least supports the standard VGA modes, it should be usable with even the most up-market of modern video adapters. It should also operate at full speed, but you may find yourself having to use the card well within its maximum resolution. In order to get the new video card "out of first gear" and obtain the best results from it, a bigger and better monitor will probably be needed as well.

In the past there were various colour and monochrome display cards that required different types of monitor. These old standards such as the MDA and CGA varieties are now obsolete, and the majority of modern PC monitors are incompatible with all these old standards. Modern PC monitors are multi-standard types that can be used in the standard 640 by 480 pixel VGA mode, plus various super-VGA modes. The number of additional modes available varies from monitor to monitor, but at least the 800 by 600 pixel mode should be supported, and most monitors can also handle 1024 by 768 pixels. The higher resolution modes such as 1280 by 1024 and 1600 x 1200 pixels are not usually available on 14 inch and 15 inch monitors. Even if these modes were available, they would be unusable. Even with the Windows "big fonts" selected, menus, etc., would be displayed too small to be really usable. In fact most PC monitors are barely usable in their highest resolution mode for this reason.

For each of the supported resolutions a monitor has a maximum refresh rate. This is simply the maximum number of complete scans of the screen that can be produced in one second. This is an important factor, because a low scan rate will produce a display that flickers quite noticeably. A display of this type is not unusable, but most users find them unpleasant to use for long periods. The minimum acceptable scan rate is a matter of opinion, but anything from about 70Hz upwards should be perfectly usable. I am reasonably happy with a 65Hz refresh rate, but at anything much less than 65Hz the picture flicker becomes very noticeable.

Some monitors, particularly the smaller budget models, use interlacing when operating at high resolutions. Interlacing is where every other line is scanned on the first frame, then the missing lines are scanned on the next frame. Two frames (i.e. two scans of the screen) are therefore needed per complete screen-full. This method is used with low scanning rates that put less stringent requirements on the components in the monitor than fast and flicker-free scan rates. Ordinary television pictures are produced using interlacing incidentally. Although the interlacing helps to minimise problems with screen flicker, it does not eliminate them. If you will be using a computer a great deal it is probably best to invest in a monitor that can provide the resolution you require without resorting to low scan rates, with or without interlacing.

When looking at monitor specifications you will often encounter the term "dot pitch". In theory, the smaller the dot pitch, the higher the display quality is likely to be. In reality matters are not as straightforward as this, and two monitors having the same claimed dot pitch might actually give significantly different display qualities. The only way to judge the quality of a display is to try it out and make a subjective judgement. The claimed size of the screen is something that is sometimes a bit over optimistic. Thankfully, some of the practices used in the past to inflate monitor sizes in specification sheets have now largely died out. If you buy a 14-inch monitor, you should not find that the diagonal measurement of the picture is actually about 11 inches. On the other hand, it will not be 14 inches either. Because the picture tube has rounded corners the usable picture size is somewhat less than the notional size. Some monitors give a larger display than others of the same specified size, but in general the actual diagonal measurement is about an inch or so less than the stated screen size.

These days virtually all monitors allow the horizontal and vertical sizes of the display to be adjusted so that it can be made to fill the screen. There should also be controls to enable the display to be accurately centred on the screen. Although you might expect two display cards operating in the same mode to position the display in more or less the same position on the screen, there can actually be quite large differences. Of more importance, the display can shift significantly when switching from one screen mode to another, and it can also expand or shrink. To avoid the need to readjust the controls each time the screen mode is altered, most monitors remember the control settings for each screen mode, and automatically switch to the appropriate set when the mode is changed. Some video adapters are supplied with a utility that enables the card to be adjusted to suit the monitor for each screen mode. Again, the appropriate settings are used when the screen mode is changed, making it unnecessary to make any manual adjustments. Monitors normally have at least one or two controls that can be adjusted to minimise various forms of distortion, and in the case of larger monitors there are often several controls of this type.

When selecting the screen resolution and scan rate in Windows 3.1 you must be careful to select a mode that is within the capabilities of your monitor. If you set a screen resolution and scan rate that is unsuitable your mistake will soon be all too obvious. When using Windows the display will either be scrambled to the point where it is totally unusable, or the monitor will simply refuse to do anything at all and will go into the standby mode. It is then a matter of re-booting into MS-DOS, running the Windows Setup program from MS-DOS, and trying again with a different display mode. With Windows 95 or 98 the "plug-n-play" feature should result in Windows detecting the new monitor and automatically making adjustments to the system settings. Failing that, the monitor should be supplied with installation software that will make the necessary changes. Any of the screen modes listed in the "Settings" section of the display Control Panel should then work properly with the new monitor.

If the monitor is not detected by Windows 95/98, and no installation software is supplied with it, one of the standard monitors available via the Control Panel should give satisfactory results. Alternatively, select any monitor that has similar characteristics to the one you are using. Windows provides a preview of new screen modes, so you should not get stuck in a video mode that the monitor can not handle. However, if this should occur, restart the computer in "safe mode" and then use the Control Panel to try a different video mode.

Modems

A modem (modulator/demodulator) enables computers to send and receive digital information over an ordinary telephone line. Until relatively recently, modems tended to be something of a minority interest, but the upsurge in interest in the Internet has now made them a standard peripheral. It has also resulted in what was once an expensive upgrade falling to prices that are well within the budget of every computer user. In the past there were numerous standards, with each generation of modems moving on to higher speeds. These earlier standards are now largely obsolete, but modern modems usually support a large range of them. As far as possible though, you should use the modem at its highest data transfer rate.

There are two general classes of modem available at present, which are the 33.6K and 56K varieties. The speed rating of a modem is simply the amount of data that it can send/receive per second. This is known as the baud rate incidentally. You will also encounter the term bits per second (BPS), which is not necessarily the same thing. Data is often compressed before it is transmitted, and then expanded again at the other end of the system. This is much the same as compressing a disc file into a ZIP file and then uncompressing it again. Compression and expansion enables data to be sent at a bit rate that is substantially higher than the baud rate.

33.6K modems will probably disappear from the market before too long, but in the mean time they represent a very low cost means of getting a computer equipped for Internet operation, and they provide reasonably fast results. The 56K modems are reliant on your local telephone exchange being a digital type (which virtually all of them are these days), and they only provide 33.6K operation when sending data. Most Internet users spend much more time downloading data than uploading it, so the fact that the modem will be slower when sending data is not a major drawback.

Confusion reined when 56K modems first appeared on the market because there were two different standards. These were (and are) the X2 and K56Flex technologies. After a long gestation period a standard for 56K modems was devised, and this is known as V90. This seems to be (more or less) an amalgam of the X2 and K56Flex technologies. If you buy a 56K modem it would be wise to obtain one that conforms to the V90 standard, or can at least be upgraded to this standard.

Modern modems invariably include a baud rate of 14.4K (the V32 bis standard) so that they can be used to send and receive faxes. You could scan in pages of text and (or) graphics and then send them as faxes, but the more usual way of using this facility is to send pages generated using a word processor, CAD program, etc. Using the computer to send faxes tends to cause confusion amongst new users, but it is actually quite straightforward. For fax transmission the modem becomes a sort of pseudo printer. You select the fax modem as the printer and then print to it in the normal way. This will run the fax software that is normally supplied with the modem, and you then select the number to dial and send the fax. The fax software can also be used to receive faxes, and in most cases it can run in the background until a fax is received. Most modems have other facilities, such as the ability to operate as an answer-phone. This type of thing is less useful than you might think, because the computer must be left running for the facility to operate. Leaving a computer running and unattended is not a good idea, since the computer represents a fire hazard.

Ins and Outs
Modems are usually available as internal or external units. On the face of it, an internal modem is the better choice for most users, as it is usually much cheaper. An internal modem is in the form of a standard expansion card, and it does not need a case,

connecting lead, or a power supply unit. These are needed for an external unit, and are largely responsible for the higher cost. There are actually one or two advantages to an external modem. One of these is simply that it can easily be moved from one computer to another if necessary. Another is that it will probably be usable with one of the PCs two existing serial ports, which makes installation much more straightforward and risk-free. In most cases the mouse will be connected to COM1, leaving COM2 free for the modem. An internal modem has its own built-in serial port, which will normally become COM3. Although a PC can have serial ports from COM1 to COM4, and parallel ports from LPT1 to LPT3, serials ports 3 and 4, and printer port 3 were not part of the original PC specification. They were added at a later date, and had to be squeezed in somehow.

Finding suitable address ranges for these ports is not usually a problem, but finding a vacant interrupt number can be. In fact it is unlikely that there will be a suitable interrupt number left unused. The generally accepted wisdom is that serial ports should have an interrupt number of no higher than seven, but if there are any unused interrupt number they are likely to be much higher than this. The way around this is for the modem's built-in serial port to share an interrupt number with another device. This is acceptable, but there are restrictions on the sharing of interrupts. This basically boils down to not using the same interrupt number for two devices that will operate simultaneously. There should be no difficulty if a modem and a soundcard share the same interrupt number, because it is unlikely that they will operate at the same time. It would not be acceptable for the modem to share the same interrupt number as the mouse or video card, as they would certainly operate simultaneously, and would both be generating interrupts at the same time.

Physically installing either an internal modem or an external unit should not present any problems. The software side of installation might just be a matter of going through the usual "plug-n-play" routine, or manually installing the drivers into

84

Windows 3.1. With an internal modem it will almost certainly involve checking the existing hardware set-up by going into Device Manager, and it might be necessary to alter some settings, or to change configuration jumpers on the modem. For the modem to work properly it is essential to avoid conflicts with existing hardware. This can all look a bit involved, but provided you follow the instruction leaflet supplied with the modem and do everything "to the letter" there should be no problems. Incidentally, if you install a SCSI card for a scanner, etc., it will probably be necessary to go through a similar routine to avoid conflicts with existing hardware. Any contentious add-on should be supplied with an instruction manual or leaflet that provides detailed installation instructions. Provided these are followed precisely, no hardware conflicts should arise.

With a 33.6K modem operating under Windows 95 you will probably have to install it as a "Standard 28.8K" modem. This worries many users, who think that their 33.6K device will be operating at something less than full speed. However, provided the baud rate for communications between the PC and the modem is set at 38.4K baud, the modem will actually operate at full speed. If no modem was fitted in the computer when Windows was installed, it is likely that some of the options associated with telephone communications will not have been installed. If you load any Internet software or other programs that require these missing Windows options, they should indicate which parts of Windows must be added. The missing parts of Windows might be installed automatically by the Setup program of the applications program, but you will probably have to run the Windows Setup program and install them manually. In Windows 95/98 it is a matter of choosing Start, Settings, Control Panel, and Add/Remove Software. Clicking on the Windows Setup tab then enables you to select the components for installation.

Soundcards
Adding a soundcard and loudspeakers should be a straightforward upgrade, since the soundcard will normally be in

the form of a PCI or ISA "plug-n-play" card. There are potential advantages in using the PCI bus for a soundcard, especially if it will be used to produce complex music sequences. Despite this, most soundcards still seem to be of the ISA variety. When using Windows 95/98 you just install the card in a vacant expansion slot, switch on, and follow any on-screen instructions that appear during boot-up. With Windows 3.1 the soundcard will have to be installed manually, and the card should be supplied with suitable drivers. A modern soundcard actually provides several functions, including sound synthesis, audio recording and playback, a MIDI interface, and a joystick interface. This means that it is typically necessary to install four sets of drivers. When installing the card into Windows 95/98 it may take a couple of reboots before all the drivers are installed and the card is ready for use. Note that it will only be possible to play audio CDs in the CD-ROM drive through the soundcard and speakers if the audio output of the CD-ROM drive is coupled to the audio input socket on the soundcard. CD-ROM drives are often supplied with a suitable cable, but if not, your local PC store should be able to supply one for a few pounds.

Although not quite a universal feature, many soundcards are equipped with an IDE interface. This feature is included because many people add a CD-ROM drive and a soundcard at the same time. This enables the PC to handle multimedia software. With a reasonably modern PC the IDE interface is not usually required, because the motherboard will have two IDE ports, with each one capable of supporting two devices. If you will not be using the IDE interface it is best to disable it, although some sound cards provide no means of switching it off. With Windows 95/98 the plug n play feature will probably insist on installing the driver for the new IDE port, and will keep reinstalling the driver if you delete it. It should install quite happily alongside the existing IDE ports, so if there is no way of removing the new port from the system you can simply ignore it. If you are installing a soundcard and CD-ROM drive into an older computer, an IDE interface on the soundcard probably represents the easiest way of interfacing the CD-ROM drive to the computer. You will need a data cable to connect the drive to the IDE port, and this is not always supplied with the drive, even if you buy the full retail boxed version. Any computer store should be able to supply a 40-way IDE cable.

If you are replacing an old CD-ROM drive it might not use an IDE (ATAPI) interface, but this is the type of drive that you will have to use as the replacement. This means abandoning the interface used for the original drive, and using an IDE type. The soundcard might have an IDE interface, or it might be possible to connect the CD-ROM drive as a slave to the hard disc. Failing that, it is a matter of trying to obtain an IDE interface card. Whatever method of interfacing is used, always remember to check that the jumpers on the drive are set for master or slave operation, as appropriate.

Newly installed soundcards often seem as though they are not working correctly. If all does not seem to be well when using Windows 95/98, go into the Control Panel and Device Manager to see if there are any exclamation marks and warning notices against the soundcard's drivers. If there are, check that the soundcard is properly pushed down into its socket. In fact it is good idea to remove the card and reinstall it in a situation of this type. Use Device Manager to delete the drivers and then reinstall them again. In most cases there will be no installation problems, and the lack of response from the card will simply be due to unsuitable settings in its control panels. From the Windows Desktop select Start, Programs, Accessories, Multimedia, and you will then be provided with a list of programs, most of which are associated with the soundcard. Try running these (particularly the Volume program) and check the numerous settings. Often the card is failing to produce any sound because its volume setting is zero, or you it might refuse to record from the microphone because it is switched to use the "line" input. If you get the control settings right, the soundcard will almost certainly operate in the required fashion.

Chapter 5

PC REPAIRS

There is an old joke about the woman who was amazed that her old broom had lasted thirty years – and it only needed two new handles and seven new heads! I suppose that the modular construction of PCs leaves them open to the same sort of claim. Over the years you can put in a new display card here, a replacement disc drive there, and maybe even a new motherboard in the fullness of time. Five or six years later the computer will still be going strong, and will probably have a specification well above that of the original machine, but the case might be the only survivor from the original hardware!

The PC's modular method of construction aids the DIY repairer. Even if you can not mend the particular item that is faulty, then it can instead be completely replaced. This might seem to be a wasteful approach, and to an extent I suppose that it is. Being realistic about modern electronics in general, current production processes are so efficient that many pieces of equipment can now be produced at very low cost. Repairing equipment can take a lot of man-hours from highly skilled (and well-paid) service engineers, making it a costly process. Modern production processes are designed to make the manufacture of equipment as cheap as possible, with servicing usually being of only secondary importance. This makes fitting replacement parts on some circuit boards quite difficult.

Obviously each case has to be assessed on its own merits. Throwing away a very high capacity hard disc drive that has become faulty just outside the guarantee period and replacing it will a new one would probably not be a cost effective way of handling the problem. At the other extreme, something like a parallel printer port card that has become faulty after several years use is probably not worth repairing. It would only cost a few pounds to replace it with a new one.

There is a big incentive to undertake DIY repairs. The cost of professional repairs on PCs can be quite high, with the minimum fee sometimes being higher than the cost of any one of an average PC's component parts. Carriage costs to and from the service centre can be high, as can calling in an engineer to provide on-site maintenance. I would not advocate prodding around inside expensive computer equipment if you are not reasonably practical, and have little knowledge about PCs. On the other hand, I think it is fair to say that a lot of PC maintenance is within the capabilities of anyone who is reasonably practical, and does know about the general make up and operation of these computers.

In this chapter we will consider some common problems with PCs (which also apply to computers in general in most cases), plus ways of detecting and correcting these faults. As already intimated, we will mainly be concerned with locating the faulty device so that it can be replaced, rather than locating and repairing the faulty module. Where appropriate, repairs on faulty sections of the computer will be described though, and the subject of preventive maintenance will also be discussed. The old saying "prevention is better than cure" is just as applicable to PCs as it is to anything else.

Hard Discs

The early hard disc drives had a reputation for very poor reliability, and in my experience the failure rate was certainly higher than for other PC components. Modern hard drives, despite the fact that they are electrically and mechanically more complex than their predecessors, seem to be much better in this respect. Problems can still occur from time to time, but fortunately most hard drives now become out of date before they become faulty. There seems to be a popular misconception that problems with hard disc drives are almost invariably due to weaknesses in the magnetic coatings of the discs themselves, and that reformatting, etc., will usually effect a cure. It is true that problems can sometimes be solved by what is basically a reformatting of the disc, and this is a subject we will pursue shortly. However, it must be pointed out that there are a fair percentage of cases where this will provide no improvement whatever. Being complex mechanical devices, hard discs are naturally prone to mechanical failures. If you take a faulty disc drive and slowly roll it over in your hands, any noise caused by bits of metal (or whatever) rattling around inside the unit almost certainly indicates that there is a serious mechanical problem with the drive.

Even if there is no evidence of anything loose inside the drive, it might still have mechanical problems. In this case, and unless there are any other signs of mechanical problems, the obvious option is to first try reformatting the drive. If this fails to effect an improvement, then the fault is almost certainly a mechanical problem with the drive. Of course, there are some complex control electronics built into every hard disc drive, and the problem could lay here. This is unlikely, as modern electronics has a very high degree of reliability. In a way it is purely academic as to whether the problem is mechanical or in the control electronics. Either way a DIY repair is certainly out of the question. You should definitely not open up a hard disc drive to look inside. These devices are sealed to keep out dust, as dust particles can easily cause serious damage to the surface of the disc if they should come between the heads and the rapidly rotating discs.

If reformatting will not effect a cure, there is little option to returning the disc drive to the dealer or manufacturer for repairs. If the disc drive is a few years old and not a very expensive type, it will certainly be better to simply fit a new drive. Getting the old one repaired (if anyone will undertake the job) would cost more, and would leave you with a well-worn disc drive. A new unit might cost a little more, but should give several years of trouble free operation. Things move on quite rapidly in the computer world, and a faulty disc drive provides a good excuse to move on to a more modern drive having a higher capacity.

While it might seem that having the old unit repaired will bring the advantage of leaving the contents of the disc intact, this is not actually the case. You might be lucky and have the disc returned with all the data and programs intact. This is unlikely though, since hard disc repairs often involve test and setting up procedures that leave the original contents of the disc largely or wholly erased. Any important data on a hard disc should always be backed-up on floppy discs, CD-ROMs, etc. Any remotely serious problem with a hard disc is almost certain to result in a total loss of the information stored on the disc.

I will not go into detail here about reformatting hard disc drives, since this is essentially the same as formatting a newly installed hard disc, which has already been described. You effectively pretend that the disc is a blank type and that you are starting from scratch with it. With the early disc drives it was possible to go right back to square one and low-level format the drive, followed by a high-level format. There could be advantages in doing this, but modern drives are supplied with the low-level formatting already done, and are not compatible with normal low-level formatting software. You are therefore limited to doing a high-level reformat using the MS-DOS FORMAT command. Although there may seem to be no point in reformatting the drive, older types can slip out of mechanical alignment slightly. Another problem that can occur is that of the magnetic signal on the disc gradually becoming weaker. Reformatting the disc will result in all the information, including track and sector marker signals, being refreshed, and returned to their original strength.

It is tempting to think of magnetic recordings of any type as being permanent. This is definitely not the case though. Although magnetic recordings seem to be long lived, they are finite, and any important information on floppy or hard disc should be refreshed at least every few years. An advantage of a digital recording, such as computer data stored on disc, is that it can be copied over and over again with no loss of quality. Provided fresh copies are made in time, data can be stored in this form indefinitely. Some people recommend periodic reformatting of hard discs and restoring of the backed-up programs and data. This is certainly a good idea, but the time involved is such that I doubt if many PC users actually bother to do this.

If the problem with the hard disc is due to the discs having developed some weak spots in their magnetic coatings, reformatting might not be much use. To sort out this type of thing some hard disc diagnostics software is required, and there is plenty of this in existence. Some computers are supplied together with some useful diagnostics utilities. In the past it was common for the BIOS to have some very useful built-in diagnostic routines, but this seems to be something of a rarity these days. If suitable software was not included with your PC, a check through some shareware/PD software catalogues will probably reveal some programs that "fit the bill". Shareware software is ideal for this type of thing since it costs you little to try it out, and you are under no legal or moral obligation to register your copy if it turns out to be of no help. Some of these programs are quite advanced, and will effectively check the disc and take any necessary action if weak spots are found. Others simply tell you if an error of some kind is found, with at least a brief run-down on the nature of the fault being provided. Windows 95/98 has some disc maintenance tools built-in, such as the Scandisc utility. The route to this is Start, Programs, Accessories, System Tools.

You can not totally rule out the possibility of the disc controller being faulty. The main control electronics for a modern hard disc drive are within the drive unit itself, but there is some electronics in the IDE controller that interfaces the drive to the rest of the PC. If this electronics fails, the hard disc will appear to be faulty. If the BIOS cannot contact the hard drive and reports that there is no device on that channel, it could be that the drive is faulty, but a fault in the IDE controller is more likely. One of the best methods of checking for faults in modular equipment is to use substitution. In this context, you could try swapping the hard disc drives of two computers. If the fault moves across from one computer to another, then the problem is clearly due to a faulty drive. If the problem persists in the PC that originally had the fault, it is this computer that is faulty. In this case it would be the IDE controller that was inoperative, and this interface is usually part of the motherboard. It might be necessary to replace the motherboard, but if the other IDE interface is working properly, operating the hard drive and CD-ROM from the other IDE controller should get the computer working again. Note that the boot drive does not have to be on IDE1, and that the computer should boot properly with the hard drive as the master unit on IDE2 provided that there are no devices connected to IDE1.

Cables

It is easy to jump to conclusions and assume that a major piece of hardware is faulty when there is another possible cause. In this case, as with many PC peripherals, there are the connecting cables to consider. Problems with cables, and not just hard disc cables, are not exactly rarities. Problems are most likely to occur with cables such as printer types, which are external to the computer. These can easily get kicked, trodden on, or otherwise disturbed, which eventually takes its toll on them. Internal cables are not immune to problems though. Bad connections can easily arise if you start delving around in the computer in order to add a new card, if you move the computer to a new location, or something of this nature. They can occasionally happen for no apparent reason whatever. This is presumably where one wire in a cable is damaged and barely making a connection. In the fullness of time it may corrode slightly, eventually resulting in its complete failure. Vibration from the cooling fans and vibration from the disc drives could presumably result in things wearing loose over a period of time, with the connection between a plug and cable eventually failing as a result.

In order to check cables some form of continuity tester is required. This can be something as basic as the old torch bulb and battery set-up at one extreme or an expensive digital multimeter set to a low resistance range at the other extreme. In either case the cables should be completely removed from the hard disc and controller (or whatever) before checking for continuity between the connectors. Modern electronic components are often delicate devices, which can be damaged by quite low voltages and currents. Fully disconnecting the cable prior to testing it ensures that there is no risk of the continuity tester damaging any of the computer's delicate electronics. If the cable is a floppy or hard disc type that has the "twist", remember that some of the connections between the connectors at the ends of the cable will be reversed.

If a cable is found to be faulty, and it is an IDC type, it will probably be possible to effect a cure by carefully removing the connectors, cutting about 20 millimetres from each end of the cable, and then refitting the connectors. Take due care when removing the connectors, as the metal terminals can tend to adhere to the wires and part company with the body of the connector, whereas it is the opposite of this that is required. This removal and replacement of the connectors might seem to be a waste of time, but it is often very effective. The most likely place for one of the wires to be damaged is where it enters the connector. Removing a connector, shortening the cable slightly, and then replacing the connector is likely to cut out the faulty piece of cable, and cure the problem. Often the cause of the fault is a poor connection between the cable and the connector. Removing the connector and refitting it tends to scrape the terminals clean, and may well clear the trouble.

I have experienced problems with disc drive cables that have connectors for two drives, where the connector for the second drive (i.e. the one that is some way in from the end of the cable) cuts through one or more of the wires. This prevents some of the signals from reaching the first drive. Continuity checks will show up this type of thing, since the connector for the second drive will not be in full electrical contact with one of the other connectors. With this type of fault it is best to obtain a new length of cable, rather than trying to repair the old one (which is never likely to be completely reliable).

Floppy Discs
Although largely mechanical in nature, modern floppy disc drives, in my experience at least, are very reliable. The same is not necessarily true of the floppy discs themselves. In fact any good quality discs from a reputable manufacturer should, unless

you are very unlucky, give trouble-free operation for a considerable period of time. Many of the cheaper discs are also of very good quality, but there are some that seem to fall short of a satisfactory level of performance. If you experience disc errors when reading from and writing to inexpensive floppy discs, but the drive shows no obvious signs of any mechanical troubles, it is likely that it is the discs are faulty and not the drive. The "acid test" is to try the drive with some good quality discs to see if any reading or writing problems are experienced with media that is known to be of a high standard.

Floppy disc drives are a good example of something where some simple preventive maintenance is well worthwhile. With floppy disc drives the recording/playback head comes into contact with the disc, as it does with ordinary audio tape and cassette recorders. In common with audio magnetic recording, this results in a certain amount of the oxide coating being rubbed off the media and onto the heads. This can build up over a period of time, resulting in both a gradual decrease in the level of the signal recorded onto the disc, and a weaker signal being read from the disc. Inevitably, this eventually results in difficulties in reading data from discs.

The use of a floppy disc drive cleaner will often result in the discs being perfectly readable again. The heads of a disc drive are often difficult to get at, especially the surfaces from which the oxide must be cleaned away. A floppy disc drive cleaner offers a quick and easy way of cleaning the heads. The type I have used successfully for some time looks very much like an ordinary floppy disc, but the disc part is actually made from an absorbent substance onto which some of the cleaning fluid (supplied as part of the cleaning kit) is placed. It is then placed in the disc drive in the usual way, and you get the computer to do several seconds worth of disc accesses (by trying to get it to list a directory for the head cleaner for instance!).

This is such a fast and simple method of cleaning the heads that it does not really make sense to wait until problems are experienced before using the cleaning kit. Cleaning the heads (say) every month or two should ensure that dirty heads do not cause any read/write problems. It should also ensure that a good strong signal is always placed onto your floppy discs, ensuring that they will remain readable for a long period of time. Some head cleaner manufacturers seem to recommend very frequent use of their products. In my experience, unless you make very intensive use of the floppy disc drives, using a cleaner only every month or two should be quite sufficient.

When dealing with old 5.25 inch discs, remember that 360K discs produced on a 1.2 megabyte drive are often not readable on a 360K drive. Many PC users have thought that a disc drive is faulty when the problem is simply that they are trying to get it to read a disc that is totally unreadable on that particular type of drive. Also remember that while a 360K drive might not be able to read a disc of this type, this does not mean that the disc is totally unreadable. 360K discs produced on 1.2 megabyte discs are usually perfectly readable on any 1.2 megabyte disc drive.

When using 5.25-inch discs make sure that you use the right type of floppy disc for each drive. As you would expect, the ordinary 360K discs (40-track, double sided, double density types) are not of a high enough standard to be used as 1.2 megabyte types. Perhaps less well appreciated is the fact that high-density 1.2-megabyte discs are not suitable for use with 360K drives. Although they have magnetic coatings of a very high standard, they are designed to take the lower power signals used by 1.2-megabyte drives. They can not properly handle the stronger signals produced by 360K drives, and tend to give an inadequate signal level when read-back by one of these drives. Always use the right type of floppy disc, not whatever happens to come to hand, or what you can get cheap at the time. Note that this problem should not occur with 3.5 inch discs, because the computer can detect whether it is a double density or high density disc in the drive. The formatting program should refuse to format the disc to the wrong capacity.

Take good care of floppy discs as they are easily damaged. Despite their name, they should definitely not be bent. 3.5 inch discs have rigid cases, which make then virtually unbendable, but the 5.25-inch varieties are quite flexible. Bending discs can result in the coating parting company with the base material, as can high or low storage temperatures (due to the base material and coating not expanding and contracting by the same amount). Writing on the label using a ballpoint pen or a hard pencil is another good way of damaging the coating!

Touching the surface of the disc can damage the coating, or result in dirt sticking to it and possibly causing damage the next time the disc is used. Again, 5.25-inch discs are much more vulnerable than the 3.5-inch type, which are fully enclosed. Dirt on the disc will not do the heads a great deal of good either. Spilling things onto a disc is a popular way of damaging them, but you might actually find that the disc is readable once it has dried out. However, if a disc becomes badly contaminated, it is advisable not to fit it into the drive at all. The contamination could easily be picked up by the heads, possibly damaging both the heads and any discs subsequently used in the drive.

Of course, magnetic fields can alter the data on the discs, and must be avoided. In the short term, only strong magnetic fields would be likely to have any effect, but note that in the long term relatively weak fields could possibly have a detrimental affect on the discs. Powerful magnets are to be found in most loudspeakers, plus virtually anything that uses a small DC electric motor. Many electrical appliances contain some form of electromagnet that produce varying magnetic fields when the device is in use, and these are probably more hazardous to floppy discs than the fixed fields produced by permanent magnets.

If the floppy disc drive is definitely faulty, and the problem is not the discs themselves, fitting a replacement should not prove to be too difficult. Floppy disc drives are now so cheap that there is no point in trying to have one repaired. If you buy one by mail order it could cost more for the postage and packing than it does for the drive itself. Provided the replacement drive is one specifically intended for PC use it should not need any changes to the configuration switches, etc. In fact it might not have any configuration switches or jumpers. Disc drive chassis have standardised mounting holes, and the original screws, mounting rails, etc., should be perfectly suitable for the new drive.

Memory

A standard feature of every PC BIOS is a set of test routines at switch-on or when the computer is reset. Some of these test routines seem to be very thorough, often taking an inordinate amount of time. Others are quite brief, but they all include a memory test (but note that this test is not run after a software reset of the Ctrl-Alt-Del type). If you go into the CMOS Setup program you may find that it is possible to select a long memory check or a more rapid one. Memory chips are highly complex devices that are generally accepted as being more prone to failure than most of the other components. The power-on self-test program will tell you if there is a problem, and it might indicate that the problem is in a particular module or bank of memory. There are diagnostic programs available which might give more help, and you should not overlook the numerous useful diagnostic programs that are in the public domain, and are readily available at very low cost from most PC public domain/shareware suppliers. The DIY PC repairer should arm himself or herself with as much diagnostic software as possible. Unfortunately, a memory problem will sometimes prevent the computer from booting-up, rendering any diagnostic software useless.

Gadgets for testing memory chips and modules are available, but are very expensive and are not a practical proposition for the DIY PC repairer. The best RAM chip tester in this context is probably the PC itself. Finding the offending module often comes down to swapping the suspect module for a new one. If that does not eliminate the problem, try swapping again with another module, and so on, until the fault is found. In the days when PC memory was provided by numerous chips on the motherboard, replacing them one at a time was a very time consuming process unless you found the faulty device early on in the proceedings. Things are much quicker with memory modules, since there are normally from one to four modules to deal with. Memory chips and modules should only be removed or inserted into their sockets when the computer is switched off. Incidentally, the same is true for expansion cards, disc drive cables, etc.

If a memory error is reported, it does not definitely mean that one of the memory chips is faulty. The problem could be due to a mechanical fault on the circuit board, but this is extremely unlikely. A much more common cause of memory problems is a memory module that is not making good contact with its socket. If a memory problem should occur, it is often worthwhile simply removing all the memory modules from their sockets, and carefully replacing them. See chapter 2 for details of fitting and removing memory modules. Ideally some contact cleaner should be used to clean the sockets before the memory chips are replaced. However, any bad contacts will almost certainly be cured simply by removing and replacing the memory modules. The main advantage of the contact cleaner is in delaying any reoccurrence of the problem.

If you try removing and reinstalling the modules you need to be reasonably careful. Memory modules are static sensitive components, and should only be handled where there is no obvious danger from high static voltages. Touch the metal chassis of the computer before you start handling memory modules, or any static-sensitive components. This should earth any static charge in your body and virtually eliminate the possibility of "zapping" the component. Make sure you refit the modules the right way round. In theory it is not possible to fit any type of memory module the wrong way round, but the flimsy holders used on some motherboards do sometimes permit this with 72-pin SIMMs.

Keyboard
I suppose that heavy users of PCs should regard keyboards as analogous to the tyres of a car: they will gradually wear out and need periodic replacement. If a keyboard has been given several years of hard use it is probably not worth repairing it, even if it is repairable. You tend to find that no sooner have you repaired one fault than another one turns up. Although a PC keyboard contains some sophisticated electronics (it actually contains its own single-chip microcomputer), keyboard problems are almost invariably due to mechanical faults. If one

part of the keyboard has sustained sufficient wear to render it inoperative, there are probably numerous other keys, etc., on the brink of developing faults.

Replacing a keyboard has to be the simplest of PC repairs. You simply unplug the old one and plug in the replacement. Virtually all current PC keyboards have the 105-key Windows 95/98 layout, but a keyboard of this type should directly replace an AT 102-key unit without any difficulty. If you are running Windows 95 or 98 on the PC, the new keyboard will probably work better than the original, with the three extra keys functioning properly. A 105-key keyboard should also work in place of an old 84-key type, but it is possible that some of the little-used keys might produce the wrong characters. It might be possible to correct this, perhaps using a keyboard remapping program, but the computer should be perfectly usable even if no remedial action is taken. Note that although XT class computers have the same 5-pin plug as AT computers, the two types are incompatible. If you require a replacement keyboard for an XT class PC you must be sure that you obtain a type that is XT compatible. Some PCs have a miniature (PS/2) keyboard connector. If you require a replacement keyboard for a PC of this type you must be careful to obtain one that has the correct type of plug, or is supplied with a suitable adapter.

Keyboards can certainly benefit from preventive maintenance and lack of abuse. A drink accidentally spilled onto a keyboard will probably ruin it, and this is not exactly an unknown occurrence. This does not necessarily leave the keyboard beyond repair, and if the actual keyboard section of the unit is removed, cleaning it in large amounts of water (preferably of the distilled variety) and thoroughly drying it may well remove all the contamination and leave it fully functional. This is likely to be a quite time consuming business though. I would recommend that no attempt should be made to dismantle the actual keyboard part of the unit. Methods of construction vary considerably from one manufacturer to another, but with many PC keyboards it is easy to end up with heaps of small springs and bits of metal, with no easy way of putting everything back together again!

The standard maintenance for a computer keyboard is to simply vacuum it every few months. This is very effective since it keeps dust and fluff away from the contacts. If any dust should get into the key-switches it can easily prevent the moving contact from touching and bridging the two fixed contacts. The switches are usually of sealed construction so that there is no easy way of dust entering, but given enough dust and a long enough period of time it is possible that problems could result. Probably a bigger danger is that so much dust and fluff will accumulate around the switch caps that their travel will be restricted to the point where some of the keys fail to make reliable contact. It is much easier never to let things build up to this point rather than to have to dig out all the fluff and dirt once things have gone too far. If the keyboard is reasonably clean, but one or two keys are unreliable, some contact cleaner squirted around the offending keys will usually clear the problem. However, it is possible that the problem is due to contact wear, and that it will return before too long. If you have to resort to the contact cleaner on a regular basis it is probably time to replace the keyboard.

If a keyboard has one or two keys that are unreliable, or one of the keys is effectively stuck in the down position, then it is virtually certain that the problem lies in the key-switches. If it simply fails to work at all, produces random characters, or something of this nature, then the problem almost certainly lies in the electronics or the connecting cable. The latter is the most likely cause of problems. Fitting a new cable is unlikely to be too difficult. Removing about half a dozen screws from the base of the unit is normally all that is needed in order to give access to the interior of the keyboard. In some cases the cable attaches to the printed circuit board via a connector, but sometimes it is necessary to desolder the five leads and then solder in the replacement.

Display and Ports

If there is a fault in the display card or monitor, this should be immediately apparent. Things are not always what they seem though, and a fault in some other part of the computer could cause a crash that would leave a blank screen, or perhaps a screen full of "garbage". Also, even if it is the display section of the computer that is at fault, it will probably not be apparent whether the problem lies in the display card or the monitor (unless there is smoke coming from the latter of course!). There are plenty of display test programs, but these are obviously only usable if the display is to some extent operational. This type of software will probably not enable you to sort out whether it is the display card or the monitor at fault.

This is another example of the substitution method of fault finding offering the best chance of finding the faulty section of the computer. If you can swap the monitors of the faulty PC and another PC, and provided the monitors are of comparable types, this will show whether it is the display card or the monitor that is faulty. If the faulty PC produces a proper display, then it is the monitor that is faulty. If the problem is not transferred to the other computer, then it is the display card that is faulty. If you are using Windows it is worth checking that the display settings are correct, and that the problem is not due to an unsuitable screen mode being used for some reason.

Most monitors and some display cards are quite expensive items. Faulty units of this type, unless they are several years old, may well be worth having repaired. Due to the rather specialised nature of display cards, the chances of repairing one successfully yourself are minimal (especially as so many of them now make extensive use of minute surface mount components). Monitors operate with extremely high voltages in parts of their circuits, and these high voltages are often retained for a long time after the unit has been switched off. This makes servicing them extremely dangerous, and something that should only be undertaken by a properly qualified service engineer. Both display cards and monitors often seem to have longer than normal guarantee periods. It is therefore worth checking the date of purchase and guarantee period even the faulty display card or monitor is a few years old.

Do not overlook the possibility that the problem is due to a faulty monitor cable. If moving the cable around and pulling on it gently results in the correct display appearing intermittently, this almost certainly indicates a faulty cable or connector. A faulty cable can also cause incorrect screen colours, with the signal for one of the primary colours not getting through to the monitor. However, this fault can also result from a faulty display card or monitor.

There are numerous pieces of software available for testing the serial and parallel ports of a PC. These operate in a variety of ways, such as sending test pieces of text to a printer, checking the registers of the ports, and getting a serial port to transmit data to itself using various baud rates and word formats. Routines of this type can be helpful, but they may not pinpoint the exact fault. Once again, the best method of tracking down the faulty piece of gear is to use the substitution method. These days the serial and parallel ports are usually provided by hardware on the motherboard, making it impractical to substitute the ports. Instead, it is a matter of trying various peripheral devices with the ports. If a peripheral device works with the port, then it is highly unlikely that the port hardware is faulty, and it is presumably one of the peripheral devices that has the problem. The on-board serial and parallel ports are controlled by the BIOS. If a port appears to be faulty it might be worthwhile checking the settings to make sure that they are correct, and that a glitch has not resulted in the suspect port being switched off. Do not forget to try substituting the connecting cables, which are probably the most likely cause of problems.

Power Supply

The power supply has to be rated as an item that is relatively likely to fail. If a PC fails to operate at all, suspect the mains lead, plug, and fuse first and only the power supply if these all seem to be all right. Ideally you should measure all the output potentials using a multimeter, to check that they are within a few percent of their rated voltages. The test meter does not need to be anything particularly fancy, and a very inexpensive type is adequate for this type of thing. It will also have resistance ranges that are useful for such things as testing fuses and leads. A simple "multimeter", as they are usually termed, is more than a little useful for anyone involved in DIY PC fault finding. These can be obtained from electronic component suppliers, and are also available from most DIY superstores.

Note that PC power supplies are of a fairly complex type known as "switch-mode" supplies. These are efficient supplies which permit the relatively high output powers required by a PC to be met by a unit that is of reasonably small dimensions. A practical consequence of using a switch-mode power supply is that it will almost certainly shut down completely (probably even cutting off the mains supply to the monitor supply outlet) unless it is connected to a load of some kind. Consequently, when the output voltages are measured the power supply unit must be connected to the motherboard and at least one disc drive.

Replacing a power supply is a fairly straightforward job. With all the leads disconnected and the four retaining screws removed from the rear panel of the computer, it should be possible to remove the faulty unit after a little careful manoeuvring. Provided the replacement is of the correct type, it should slide into place without too much difficulty, and the four fixing screws for the original power supply should fit the new one. However, PC power supplies have been produced in a variety of shapes and sizes, and you therefore need to make sure that a replacement power supply has the correct physical characteristics, as well as the correct power rating. Provided your PC does not have an unusual style of case, and it is not extremely old, it should be possible to obtain a suitable replacement. It is not essential to use a supply having a rating that is identical to that of the original unit. Provided it has a rating that is equal to or higher than that of the original supply unit there should be no problems. If your PC has an ATX style case and motherboard, it will require an ATX style power supply unit, and not an ordinary AT type. If your PC is in some way non-standard and it is not possible to obtain a suitable replacement, the only alternative is to buy a new case and power supply unit, and to rebuild the computer in the new case. This will be somewhat more time consuming than simply replacing the power supply unit, but it is unlikely to cost much more.

As much of the power supply's circuitry is connected direct to the mains supply, do not try removing the metal covers and delving around inside. To do so could risk sustaining a very dangerous electric shock, and would be unlikely to effect a repair. Power supply failures usually result in substantial damage to its components, and it is not usually worthwhile attempting repairs anyway.

Safe and Sound

Soundcards seem to be one of the more troublesome PC components, but this has nothing to do with hardware reliability. Obviously soundcards can become faulty, but most problems with these cards lie in the software. A common problem is that of the control settings becoming altered for no apparent reason. The volume control mysteriously sets itself at minimum, you find that you can no longer record from the microphone because it has been switched off, and this sort of thing. This type of problem often seems to occur after new software has been installed, or when Windows has been updated in some way. If there is a problem with the soundcard it is always a good idea to run the Windows programs associated with it (look in the multimedia accessories) to see if the control settings have been altered. You can also check the settings in the multimedia section of the control panel.

When using Windows 95/98 there can be problems with the software drivers. It is worth looking at the entries for the soundcard in Device Manager to see if the are any exclamation marks and warning messages. Some cards tend to suffer from occasional problems with extra copies of the drivers being installed. This is presumably due the "plug-n-play" feature going slightly astray at times. Whatever the cause, with two copies of a driver installed the normal result is that neither of them will function properly. Deleting the drivers and reinstalling then may effect a cure, but you may simply find that the damaged drivers are reinstated. The safer method is to delete the drivers from within Device Manager, switch off the computer, and remove the soundcard from the computer. Reboot the computer and then shut it down and switch off again. Then reinstall the soundcard and drivers. This should "fool" the computer into starting the installation "from scratch", and with luck fully operational versions of the drivers will be installed. If problems of this type persist you should consult the manufacturer of the card, as there may be updated drivers available. Consulting the relevant web site is often the quickest way of sorting out a problem of this type.

General
When a PC has been in use for a year or two it will sometimes start to produce intermittent faults, such as the odd disc problem, the display failing to operate, or ports not responding properly. This could be due to faults in various parts of the computer, but this type of general and intermittent failure often seems to be the result of bad contacts between the various modules in the system. Modular construction certainly has its advantages, but there is a definite drawback in the form of numerous non-soldered connections all over the system.

If problems of the this type should occur, the cure is to take out the expansion cards, disconnect all the cables, give everything a clean with switch or contact cleaner, and then reassemble everything. It is not a bad idea to give the computer this treatment annually anyway, rather than waiting for the occasional error message to be produced before taking any action. Taking out the expansion cards, disconnecting all the hard and floppy disc leads, etc., and then reassembling everything is not exactly a high-tech job. On the other hand, it is very easy to forget which way round leads connect, and things of this nature.

To avoid possible problems when reassembling the computer, it is advisable to make notes and, if necessary, quick sketches before taking it apart. In particular, if there are two identical connectors, make sure you know where to reconnect each one. If necessary, put identifying marks on cables or connectors so that there is no risk of getting them swapped over later on. Most computer connectors are polarised types so that there is no risk of fitting them the wrong way round. However, there are plenty of exceptions and you should make a note of the correct orientation for any non-polarised connectors. You will often find that pin numbers are marked on connectors, making the correct orientation obvious. In some cases you will need quite a powerful magnifier in order to read the numbers, which are often moulded into a plastic part of the connector in minute lettering.

When giving the system a clean of this kind, do not ignore parts such as printer and keyboard leads. Disconnecting these and cleaning both connectors should help to keep the system in good and error-free operation.

Chapter 6

RESURRECTING AN OLD PC

One reason for the success of PCs is undoubtedly their modular construction, which makes it easy to add new features such as CD writers, or to upgrade existing facilities. If your video card is not up to the latest 3-D games, you can simply remove it and fit the latest high-speed 3-D video card instead. If the hard disc drive no longer has sufficient capacity for the latest mega-powerful software suites, it can be replaced with a higher capacity drive that will provide you with all the storage space you could possibly want. In theory, you can go on upgrading a PC forever, keeping it fully up-to-date with all the latest "bells and whistles". In practice there is a limit to the length of time that you can continue with this form of gradual upgrading. Eventually the basic PC becomes so out of date that it can no longer accommodate the latest PC peripherals, etc. This obsolescence occurs due to the changes in the PC interfaces, and there can also be problems with the BIOS when trying to use the latest gadgets in an old PC.

Does this mean that a PC can not go on indefinitely? Not really, it just means that after a number of years a major upgrade will be required in order to keep the computer up to date. When considering any major upgrade you first need to ask yourself whether or not it is worth upgrading the computer at all. If the answer is yes, you then have to work out exactly what you are going to replace, and what you are going to replace it with. Deciding whether or not a computer is worth upgrading is to some extent a subjective matter. If you have a computer based on a 80386 or 80486 micro-processor that has been kept up to date with multimedia add-ons, a high-capacity hard disc drive, etc., you have an ideal candidate for a major upgrade. The PC has plenty of modern components that will work well in a "new" computer. At the other extreme, a PC of similar vintage that is still in its original form is unlikely to be worth upgrading. It would actually be possible to bring a computer of this type up to a modern specification, but so much would have to be changed and added that very little of the original PC would remain in the upgraded computer. In all probability only the floppy drive, case and power supply unit would be carried through to the "new" computer. It might also be possible to use the keyboard, mouse, and monitor with the upgraded machine, but the input devices are likely to be well worn, and the monitor might not do justice to a modern PC.

People sometimes ask me for advice about upgrading 80286 PCs, or even earlier XT class computers. With computers of this vintage it is probably not worthwhile attempting to give them a major upgrade. My advice is to continue using computers such as these with their original software rather than trying to get them to run modern programs. Adding more memory and other easy fixes will not enable a ten year old PC to run modern software. The only viable alternative is to build a new PC "from scratch" using any modern components that can be salvaged from the old PC. Unfortunately, in most cases there will be little or nothing that can be usefully moved on into the new computer.

Ringing the Changes
If you have a PC that is worthy of a major upgrade, just what has to be changed in order to bring it up to a modern specification? In an ideal world you would simply compare the current specification of the PC with the specification of the PC that you would like. You would then replace anything in the current machine that fell short of your requirements. In the real world this could well cost very much more than you are prepared to spend on the project. If financial restrictions dictate the implementation of a minimal upgrade, it will still be necessary to replace much of the existing PC. The obvious way of providing a PC with an increase in speed is to upgrade the processor. Unfortunately, it is not possible to simply remove an 80386 or 80486 microprocessor and replace it with a modern Pentium type. Older processors are physically and electrically incompatible with modern Pentium devices.

Indeed, upgrading from an early Pentium processor to a modern type often involves much more than simply swapping the processor and re-configuring the motherboard. There are two main problems when attempting a Pentium-to-Pentium upgrade. One of these is simply the physical and electrical difference between early and modern Pentium processors. The 60 and 66 MHz Pentium processors require motherboards fitted with a socket known as "Socket 4", whereas more recent Pentiums require "Socket 7" equipped motherboards. Pentium II processors do not have a conventional socket at all, and fit into what looks more like a socket for a memory module than an integrated circuit holder. This is known as a "Slot 1" connector. Yet more slots and sockets are planned for future PC microprocessors.

The other potential problem is that the motherboard of your computer may not support faster Pentium processors even if it has the right type of socket. If these faster processors were not available at the time computer was built, it would be unreasonable to expect the motherboard to support them. The manual for the motherboard should provide details of the processors that are supported, together with details of how to reconfigure the board for each of these chips. It is important to realise that support for the faster "classic" (non-MMX) Pentium processors does not mean that a motherboard can be used with MMX chips having the same clock frequency. The problem here is that the MMX versions operate from dual supply voltages, whereas the non-MMX processors operate from a single supply rail. In the motherboard manuals the single and dual supply interfaces are often referred to as "P54C" and "P55C" respectively. Unless the manual specifically states that the motherboard supports P55C/MMX processors, it is not suitable for use with any make of MMX class processor.

Although it is not possible to fit an ordinary modern Pentium processor into an old 80486 or Pentium motherboard, there are various "Overdrive" processors that can be used to pep up an old PC. At one time these were quite expensive, and in many cases it was actually cheaper to buy a new motherboard and conventional processor rather than an equivalent "Overdrive" style processor. These days the prices of upgrade processors are much more reasonable and they represent a more practical alternative to a major upgrade. If you require more speed but are unwilling to undertake a complete rebuild of the PC, apart from buying a new computer there is probably no alternative to using an upgrade processor. However, bear in mind that you are only gaining an increase in processing speed, and that the rest of the system remains unchanged. Upgrading to a more modern motherboard often brings a small but worthwhile improvement in speed, together with other advantages such as a more modern BIOS and the ability to take more and faster memory. A change in motherboard can also provide more modern interfaces such as the USB (universal serial bus) and the AGP (advanced graphics port) varieties. Additional time and effort put into a motherboard upgrade is likely to be well rewarded.

Lost Memory

Changing the motherboard is likely to enforce other changes, such as the fitting of new memory. 80386 and 80486 based PCs mostly have their memory in the form of 30-pin SIMMs (single in-line memory modules), but Pentium motherboards invariably require either 72-pin SIMMs or 168-pin DIMMs (dual in-line memory modules). Some of the later 80486 motherboards do actually use 72-pin SIMMs, and it may be possible to use these with the new motherboard. However, many of the latest motherboards, especially the Pentium II variety, can only use the 168-pin modules. If you wish to reuse existing 72-pin SIMMs you must therefore be careful to choose a motherboard that supports this type of memory. This is likely to preclude an upgrade to one of the most modern Pentium processors.

With the current low price of memory it would probably be advisable to scrap the existing memory and upgrade to more modern memory modules that will enable the computer to reach its full potential. It is also worthwhile increasing the amount of memory so that the upgraded computer can run modern operating systems and applications software properly. There are actually devices called "SIMM savers" which enable 30-pin memory modules to be used with motherboards that have sockets for the 72-pin variety. Again, with the current low price of modern memory modules there would seem to be little point in using them. The cost of the adapters could easily exceed the cost of replacing the memory modules!

The video adapter is another likely problem area when undertaking a major upgrade. If the existing video card is a PCI type, there should be no difficulty in using it in one of the PCI expansion slots of the new motherboard. On the other hand, if the existing video card requires a VESA expansion slot there is no chance of using it with a modern motherboard. This type of interface is now obsolete, and no current motherboards are equipped to deal with any form of VESA expansion card. The situation is similar if the existing video adapter is an ISA type. Although ISA expansion slots may be phased out in the not too distant future, I have yet to see a PC motherboard that does not include at least two of these. It might actually be possible to get an ISA video card to work properly in a modern PC, but it is unlikely to be worth the effort. The best video cards of a few years ago are quite slow when compared to most of the cheaper boards that are available today. Discarding the old video adapter and replacing it with an inexpensive modern type is likely to give a large increase in performance. If you are heavily into any form of graphics application it would almost certainly be worthwhile upgrading to one of the modern high-speed video cards. These can greatly increase the operating speed of many heavyweight graphics applications.

Last, but by no means least, bear in mind that all modern Pentium class processors require a heatsink and fan in order to ensure that there is no danger of the processor overheating. Even if the existing processor is equipped with a heatsink and (or) cooling fan, this is unlikely to be of any use with the new processor. Some Pentium class processors require larger heatsinks and more efficient fans than others, and when ordering the processor it is important to ensure that you obtain an adequate cooling system for it. It is advisable to buy the

113

heatsink and fan at the same time as you buy the processor. Any reputable PC component supplier should know exactly what is and is not suitable for each processor that they sell, and should be able to supply you with a suitable heatsink and fan.

It has to be admitted that changing the processor, motherboard, video card, and memory of a PC means replacing a high percentage of the computer. While this is certainly not going to be cheap, when you look at the advantages gained it could be regarded as "cheap at the price." In days gone by people often used to spend quite large sums of money in order to obtain an increase in speed of about 30 to 50 percent. By upgrading an old 80386 or 80486 based PC into something like a 233 MHz MMX type you are likely to gain roughly a tenfold increase in speed. A computer that could previously not operate satisfactorily with modern software, if it could run it at all, will be transformed into one that will work well with practically any current software title. Even if you are upgrading an early Pentium based PC, the increase in speed provided by a more modern Pentium is likely to be quite surprising.

Hard Choices
The hard disc drive tends to be one of the weakest points of older PCs. Although the speed of data transfers tends to be quite slow by current standards, the level of performance obtained is usually just about adequate for modern software. It is the amount of storage capacity available that is the main problem. Older PCs generally have hard disc capacities of around 100 to 300 MB, whereas modern PCs usually have hard discs with about 20 times this capacity. Old disc drives are adequate for MS-DOS programs, and possibly for Windows 3.1 software, but are inadequate for Windows 95 and 98. If you are upgrading a PC that still has its original hard disc drive, and you will need to run a modern operating system such as Windows 98 on the upgraded machine, a new hard drive may well be essential. Apart from its slow speed and limited capacity, there has to be a question mark over the reliability of any hard disc drive that is more than about five years old. Unless you are very

unlucky, a new hard disc drive should operate reliably and keep your data safe for many years to come.

Fortunately, like virtually all computer hardware, hard disc drives are now relatively inexpensive and upgrading to a new bigger and better unit should not "cost the earth". Apart from a massive increase in capacity, a modern hard disc drive should also provide a worthwhile increase in operating speed. Virtually all modern motherboards and IDE hard discs support UDMA33 operation, and together with improvements in modern hard drives this provides a very substantial increase in performance over older drive units. Of course, if the PC has been fitted with a replacement drive, or has had a hard disc upgrade at some time in the not too distant past, it will be better able to handle modern operating system and software. If the "new" drive is more than a few years old it would still be worthwhile having serious thought about fitting a new one.

Protection Racket

Those readers who are used to dealing with electronic components will no doubt be aware that most computer components are vulnerable to damage by static electricity. They will also be used to handling static-sensitive components and taking the necessary precautions to protect them from damage. For the benefit of those who are not familiar with these precautions I will outline the basic steps necessary to ensure that no components are accidentally "zapped". I think it is worth making the point that it does not take a large static charge complete with sparks and "cracking" sounds to damage sensitive electronic components. Large static discharges of that type are sufficient to damage most semiconductor components, and not just the more sensitive ones. Many of the components used in computing are so sensitive to static charges that they can be damage by relatively small voltages. You can "zap" these components simply by touching them, and in most cases would not be aware that anything had happened.

When handling any computer components you should always keep well away from any known or likely sources of static electricity. This includes such things as computer monitors, television sets, any carpets or furnishings that are known to be prone to static generation, and even pets that are known to get charged-up fur coats. Also avoid wearing any clothes that are known to give problems with static charges. This seems to be less of a problem than it once was, because few clothes these days are made from a cloth that consists entirely of man-made fibres. There is normally a significant content of natural fibres, and this seems to be sufficient to prevent any significant build-up of static charges. However, if you should have any garments that might give problems, make sure that you do not wear them when handling any computer equipment or components.

Electronics and computing professionals often use quite expensive equipment to ensure that static charges are kept at bay. Most of these are not practical propositions for amateur computer enthusiasts or those who only deal with computers professionally on a very part-time basis. If you will only be working on computers from time to time, some very simple anti-static equipment is all that you need to ensure that there are no expensive accidents. When working on a motherboard it is essential to have some form of conductive worktop that is earthed. These can be purchased from the larger electronic component suppliers, but something as basic as a large sheet of aluminium cooking foil laid out on the workbench will do the job very well. The only slight problem is that some way of earthing the foil must be devised. The method I generally adopt is to connect the foil to the metal chassis of a computer using a crocodile clip lead. Crocodile clips are available from electronic component suppliers, as are sets of made-up leads. The computer that acts as the earth must be plugged into the mains supply so that it is earthed via the mains earth lead. The computer should be switched off, and the supply should also be switched off at the mains socket.

If you wish to make quite sure that your body remains static-free, you can earth yourself to the computer by way of a proper earthing wristband. This is basically just a wristband made from electrically conductive material that connects to the earth via a lead and a high value resistor. The resistor does not prevent any static build-up in your body from leaking away to earth, but it will protect you from a significant shock if a fault should result in the earthing point becoming "live". If you do not want to go to the expense of buying a wristband, a simple but effective alternative is to touch the conductive worktop from time to time. This will leak away any gradual build-up of static electricity before it has time to reach dangerous proportions.

Decisions, Decisions

Having decided to upgrade an old PC, the next step is to choose the processor. If you wish to keep things as simple as possible, choose a processor that will fit the existing motherboard. Although a basic upgrade of this type has obvious attractions it also limits the increase in performance. As explained previously, in the most cases it will be necessary to opt for some form of "Overdrive" processor, as it is unlikely that any normal Pentium class processor will be compatible with the motherboard. If you are upgrading a relatively recent PC it might be possible to fit a faster Pentium processor, and it is a matter of consulting the motherboard's manual to determine which processors it supports. One potential problem here is that any faster processor that will fit the motherboard might already be obsolete and difficult to obtain. Most obsolete processors are still available, but are mainly sold as "spares" and at spare-part prices. A new budget processor and motherboard could well be a better option.

Using an "Overdrive" style processor is very straightforward, and in most cases there will be no need to change the configuration of the motherboard. You have to do little more than unplug the old processor and fit the new one. Processors of this type are normally supplied with detailed fitting instructions, and in the case of 80486 upgrade processors, an extraction tool for the old processor is normally provided as well. Note that it is impossible to upgrade a processor that is soldered direct to the motherboard rather than being fitted in socket. Most 80486 chips are fitted to the motherboard via a socket, but some are soldered to the board. This point should obviously be checked before buying an upgrade processor. Provided the new chip is in good condition and has no bent pins, it should fit into its holder using nothing more than moderately firm pressure. The only complication is that 80486 chips are square, and will fit into the holder with any of the four possible orientations. You therefore need to be careful that pin one as marked on the chip itself matches up with pin one on the holder. The instruction leaflet provided with the processor usually explains in great detail how to find pin one of the processor and pin one of the socket. Pin one of the processor is normally indicated by a chamfered corner on the chip itself, and by an extra pin on the socket (see Figure 6.1). There will probably be some markings on the motherboard which also indicate pin one of the socket.

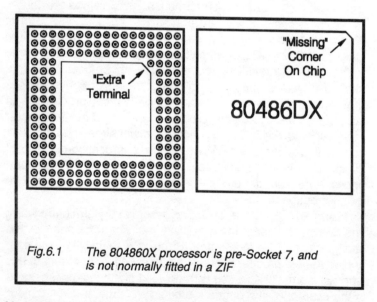

Fig.6.1   The 804860X processor is pre-Socket 7, and is not normally fitted in a ZIF

No extraction tool is required for Pentium chips as they are fitted into ZIF (zero insertion force) sockets. There should be a small lever along one side of the socket. Pull the handle of the lever

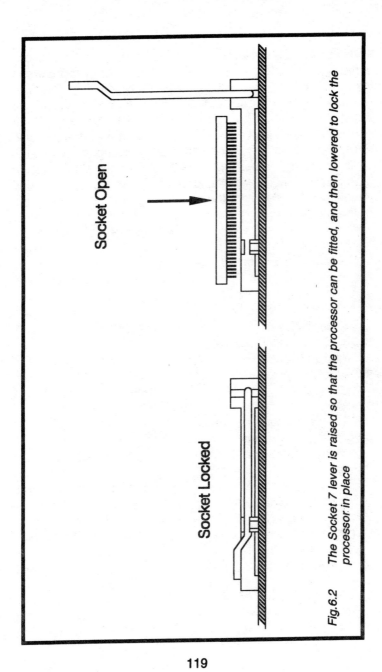

Fig.6.2   The Socket 7 lever is raised so that the processor can be fitted, and then lowered to lock the processor in place

slightly away from the socket and then raised the handle to a vertical position (Figure 6.2). The processor should then pull free from the socket without any difficulty. Fitting the new processor is basically just a matter of reversing this process. Fit the processor into its holder being careful not to bend any of the pins. Once the chip is correctly aligned with the socket it should easily drop-down into place and should not require any force. Unlike a 80486 processor, Pentium chips have a missing pin that prevents them from fitting into the holder with the wrong orientation. If you look at the processor you will notice that one of the four corner pins is missing, and that the corresponding hole in the socket is also absent. Provided you match the "missing" pin and the "missing" hole, the chip should drop down into place without difficulty, but it can be a bit fiddly getting the two correctly aligned. Once the processor is in place the lever on the socket is returned to the horizontal position. This should lock the processor firmly in place.

"Overdrive" processors are normally supplied complete with a built-on heatsink and fan. Pentium chips are sometimes supplied complete with a matching heatsink and cooling fan, but these are normally optional extras. It is not a good idea to try using any heatsink and (or) cooling fan that was fitted to the old processor, as this is unlikely to be adequate for the new chip. If no cooling system is supplied as standard with the new processor, order a matching heatsink and fan when you buy the new chip, and get an assurance that the cooling system is up to the task.

The cooling fan will require a 12-volt supply, and there are two normal ways of obtaining this. The most common method is to obtain power from one of the 5.25-in. disc drive supply outputs of the power supply unit. There will not always be a spare output of this type, but the fan will almost certainly be fitted with a lead that has two connectors. One of these connects to the output of the power supply and other connects to a 5.25-in. drive. This enables a single output of the power supply to provide power to both the cooling fan and one of the drives. The alternative method is to power the fan from the motherboard. Virtually all modern motherboards have a small two-pin connector that can supply 12 volts to the cooling fan. In practice this is likely to be a much simpler and easier way of doing things, but you are unlikely to be supplied with a fan that has the right type of connector. Tapping off power from a disc drive is a method that can be applied to any PC, and most fans are therefore equipped with this "safe" method of connection.

All Change

The pace of modern technology is such that a processor upgrade, even for a computer that is only a year or two old, often means changing the motherboard. Except for those who require the ultimate in performance, it is now the norm to buy a computer that has a "bog standard" microprocessor, but a motherboard that will take the latest super-fast processor. This enables the computer to be easily upgraded to a faster processor at a later date when the super-fast processor has come down to a more reasonable price. This is fine in theory, but things move on so rapidly that once you are ready to upgrade you may well find that the super-fast processor has become obsolete. Even if it is still available you may not feel that it no longer represents a worthwhile upgrade.

Many PC users are understandably rather reluctant to attempt an upgrade that involves changing the motherboard. In truth, it is not really that difficult, but things can go wrong. If you buy a new computer or pay someone to perform a major upgrade for you, presumably you will be covered by some form of guarantee, and the risk will be minimal. When performing upgrade yourself you are covered to some extent by the guarantees for the new components that are being added. On the other hand, if you make a mess of things and damage one or more of the components, these guarantees will be of no help and you have to take responsibility for this type of thing yourself. It is only fair to point out that even if you get everything just right there is still an outside chance that the finished computer will fail to work absolutely perfectly. PCs are notorious for obscure incompatibility problems, and although it is fair to say that

121

problems of this type are quite rare, they remain a very real possibility.

Looking at things realistically, the chances of damaging one of the components are quite small provided you take the necessary anti-static handling precautions and do not go at things like the proverbial "bull in china shop". PC components are not ultra-delicate, but if you start forcing things into place you may well seriously damage one or more of the parts. The cost of repairing PC components tends to be greater than they are worth, so if something should become damaged it will probably be a write-off. However, provided you proceed carefully and patiently it is highly unlikely that any of the components will come to grief. Problems with hardware incompatibility are unlikely, but provided you have more than one PC they can usually be dealt with quite easily anyway. Some swapping of components between two computers will usually solve any problems of this type. If you only have one PC, performing a major upgrade on it is slightly more risky, but I do not think that I would let that deter me.

If you do decide to go ahead with an upgrade that involves changing the motherboard the first act is to choose your new processor. It is then a matter of choosing a motherboard to suit this processor. You must be careful to choose one that has the correct form factor for the case you are using. There are two styles of board, which are the AT and ATX varieties. The AT style boards are what could be regarded as traditional PC motherboards, and these are based on the layout used in the original IBM AT PCs. Things have moved on, and although modern motherboards include many features that were once implemented via add-on cards, they are invariably much smaller than the original board. These are often referred to as "baby AT" boards in advertisements. Their dimensions vary somewhat from one board to another, but their overall size and the positions of the mounting holes should be along the general lines of Figure 6.3.

The original AT board had provision for three more mounting holes along the front edge of the board, but due to the reduced

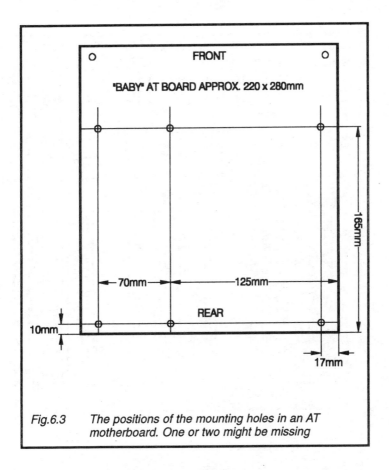

FRONT

"BABY" AT BOARD APPROX. 220 x 280mm

165mm

←70mm→ ←125mm→

REAR

10mm

17mm

Fig.6.3   *The positions of the mounting holes in an AT*
            motherboard. One or two might be missing

size of modern motherboards these are usually absent. If there
are any mounting holes here they will probably not match up
with any fixing points in the case, and are normally just ignored.
Note that all six of the main mounting holes may not be present,
and that these days most boards only have five of them. ATX
boards are much wider than the AT type, but have a much
smaller front-to-back measurement. The main point of this
layout is that it leaves the area in front of the expansion slots
free from any large obstructions, making it possible to fit full-

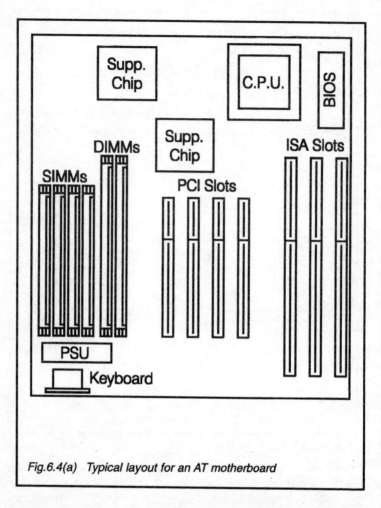

Fig.6.4(a) Typical layout for an AT motherboard

length cards into any expansion slot. Full-length cards can cause major problems with AT motherboards, which generally have the processor in front of the expansion slots. This did not cause any problems with the original AT computers because they did not have a heatsink and fan fitted to the microprocessor. All modern Pentium processors require a

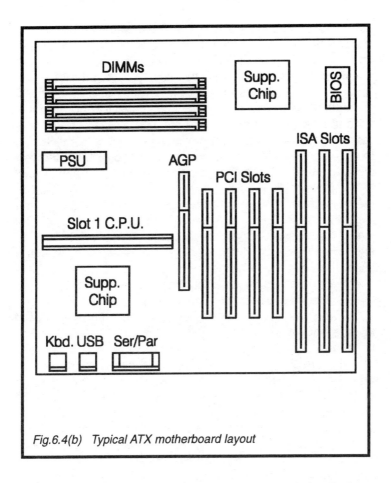

DIMMs

Supp. Chip

BIOS

ISA Slots

PSU

AGP

PCI Slots

Slot 1 C.P.U.

Supp. Chip

Kbd. USB Ser/Par

Fig.6.4(b)   Typical ATX motherboard layout

heatsink and fan, and this cooling system protrudes well above the top of the processor. This effectively makes the processor much higher and partially obscures at least two expansion slots and probably more. Figures 6.4(a) and (b) show typical AT and ATX board layouts.

Another difference between AT and ATX motherboards is their power supply requirements. An AT board requires supplies of plus and minus 5 volts, and plus and minus 12 volts. An AT power supply has two leads terminated in separate connectors that fit side-by-side on a large connector on the motherboard. The supply requirements of an ATX motherboard are similar, but it additionally requires a +3.3 volt supply. Also, an ATX power supply has a single lead and connector to couple its output to the motherboard. There is another important difference between AT and ATX motherboards, and this is that ATX style boards have the connectors for such things as serial and parallel ports mounted on the board. These match up with cut-outs in the rear of the case, much like the keyboard connector of any normal PC. With AT motherboards the port connectors are mounted on the rear of the case, or on blanking plates fitted behind vacant expansion slots. The connectors are supplied fitted with "flying" leads that connect to the motherboard. Modern PCs tend to have large numbers of cables going here there and everywhere inside the case. The ATX method of handling the standard ports has the advantage of reducing the number of cables, which makes it much easier to work on the interior of the unit.

AT and ATX motherboards have such different shapes and layouts that you should be in no doubt which is used in your PC. It is only fair to point out that some of the larger PC manufacturers do not always use one of the standard layouts, and a major upgrade to any non-standard PC may well be impossible. Only proceed with an upgrade if you are sure that your PC is one of the standard types. Unless you are upgrading a computer that is relatively recent it will almost certainly have an AT style case and power supply. The practical importance of this is that it will only accept AT style motherboards, and is totally unusable with ATX boards. This is not a major limitation at present because AT style motherboards are available for practically all modern Pentium processors. Most AT motherboards have both AT and ATX style power supply connectors, and can be used in the majority of ATX cases. As there is now such a large range of ATX motherboards available there would seem to be no point in doing this, and if you are upgrading a PC that has an ATX case I would strongly recommend using a motherboard of the same type.

Having obtained the new processor, a matching heatsink and fan, and a suitable motherboard, you can then move onto any other components that need to be upgraded. As pointed out previously, it will almost certainly be necessary to obtain new memory modules and a new video card. It is a good idea to obtain the motherboard before deciding on the type of memory to use. The manual for the motherboard should make it clear which type or types of memory are supported. There is a chapter of this book that deals specifically with memory matters, and this material will not be repeated here. Consult the relevant chapter if you are unsure about the differences between the various types of memory that are available. With video cards it is mainly a case of you get what you pay for, with the more expensive boards providing faster operation. However, even the cheaper video cards provide good 2-D performance and support high-resolution modes with lots of colours. One of these cards should be perfectly all right for general-purpose use with Windows software. If you are heavily into graphic software or games it will probably be worthwhile investing in one of the more expensive 2-D/3-D boards. With the more up-market video cards you often have the choice of an ordinary PCI type or an AGP (advanced graphics port) card. In general, AGP cards are faster than the ordinary PCI variety, especially with 3-D graphics. The PCI expansion bus operates at 33MHz, but the AGP bus is a 66MHz type (with faster versions planned). If you wish to use an AGP card make sure you obtain a motherboard that has an interface of this type, as they are far from universal at present.

Nuts and Bolts
Having collected together the parts for the upgrade, the next step is to open up the PC and remove the old motherboard. The manual for your computer should give details of how to remove the outer casing, but this usually just involves removing three or four screws the rear of the case. With most cases the top and sides are a single piece of metal which can then be slid backwards and away from the main case. With some older PCs the front fascia is also part of the removable outer casing, and

with these the outer casing is removed by pulling it forwards and away from the main unit. With cases of this type the retaining screws might be on the underside of the case rather than at the rear.

Before the motherboard can be removed it must be disconnected from the power supply, loudspeaker, on/off LED, etc. The expansion cards must also be removed. Depending on the type of case involved and the number of drives fitted, it might be necessary to remove one or more of the disc drives in order to permit removal of the motherboard. If you are upgrading the hard disc drive you may wish to remove the old unit. However, if the case can accommodate both hard drives it may be as well to leave the old unit in place, and operate the computer with two hard drives. In the long-term you will probably wish to phase out the old drive, but initially it can be useful to include it in the computer. Having the two drives operating side-by-side makes it easy to copy files from the old drive to the new one. Where possible, leave the data cables connected to the drives. If the cables are found to seriously impede work on the computer they must be completely disconnected and removed. It is then advisable to make some simple sketches or notes so that there is no difficulty in reconnecting them correctly.

You may find that removing the old motherboard simply requires five or six screws to be undone, and that the board will then lift clear of the chassis. With most boards though, there will only be one or two screws to remove. The board will still be held in place by a number of plastic stand-offs, but in most cases it can be slid sideways and then clear of the chassis. The plastic stand-offs will still be attached to the motherboard, and must be removed so that they can be used with the new board. This requires the tops of the stand-offs to be squeezed inwards using a pair of pliers and then pulled free of the board (Figure 6.5). If the motherboard can not be slid free from the chassis, you may find that the stand-offs can be released on the underside of the case. They may fit into the chassis in much the same way that they fit into the motherboard, or they may be held in place with fixing screws. The construction of some PC cases is such that it

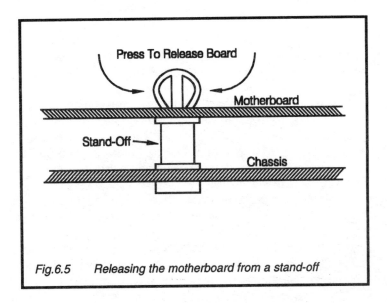

Press To Release Board

Motherboard

Stand-Off

Chassis

Fig.6.5   Releasing the motherboard from a stand-off

may not be possible to free the stand-offs from the case. You then have the task of removing the motherboard with the stand-offs still fixed to the case. This tends to be rather awkward because the motherboard is likely to be somewhat inaccessible, and there is also a tendency for one stand-off to slip back into place while you are freeing the next one. You may need a helper to hold the board and prevent it from slipping back into place while you unclip the stand-offs. Alternatively, you could try improvising some simple wedges to prevent the board from dropping back into place.

Pre-Fabrication
It is advisable to do as much work as possible on the motherboard before it is mounted in the case, because it is far more accessible when it is on the worktop. The amount of setting up required varies greatly from one board to another, and with some boards there is no need to bother with any form of configuration switches or jumpers. The correct clock frequency and processor supply voltages are set using the BIOS Setup

program when the computer is run for the first time. In most cases the BIOS will automatically detect the processor type and configure the board accordingly. You only need to intervene if the BIOS makes a mistake or you wish to use over-clocking techniques in an attempt to improve performance.

If the motherboard has hardware rather than software configuration, it will be necessary to set up either a DIP switch or a number of jumpers to produce the correct operating conditions for the processor. A DIP switch is simply a bank of small switches mounted on the motherboard, and there will normally be either eight or 10 switches. Jumpers are simply small pieces of metal that are normally encased in plastic, and they are used to bridge pins on the motherboard. The pins may be grouped together in a single bank, but they are usually scattered around the board in small groups. The motherboard's manual should give details of how to set up the DIP switches or jumpers to suit each of the supported processors.

It is not essential to understand what you are doing when you configure the motherboard, but it can often be helpful. It is necessary to set a suitable clock frequency for the processor, but this is not as straightforward as you might think. Although the processor will probably be operating at around 200MHz or more, the motherboard and memory will be operating at a much lower frequency. The original Pentium motherboards operated with a maximum system frequency of just 66MHz, and (say) a 233MHz Pentium is accommodated by running the processor at 3.5 times the board clock frequency. At the time of writing this, most motherboards still operate at 66MHz even when they are fitted with processors that require clock frequencies of 300MHz or more. This huge discrepancy between the system and processor clock frequencies is clearly undesirable as it reduces the increase in speed provided by a super-fast processor. The processor tends to spend much of its time waiting for everything else to catch up. Some of the more recent processors are designed for used in motherboards that operate at a higher system clock rate of 100MHz. These are the Pentium II and Xeon processors (the ones having clock speeds of 350MHz or more) and the AMD K6-2 3D Now! chips. No doubt more chips of this type will follow. Faster system clock frequencies give significantly better results with faster processors, but these high system clock frequencies can only be used with processors that are designed to handle them.

Matters are further complicated by the fact that the quoted clock speed of some processors is slightly different to the frequency actually used. With some versions of the Cyrix/IBM 200MHz MMX chip for example, the motherboard operates at 75MHz with the processor clocked at twice this frequency. This obviously gives an actual processor clock frequency of just 150MHz and not 200MHz. The reason for this discrepancy is that the manufacturer quotes an equivalent clock frequency rather than the actual clock rate. In other words, although the chip has a clock frequency of 150MHz, in terms of performance it is roughly equivalent to a 200MHz MMX Pentium processor. As many readers will no doubt have noticed, the system clock frequency of 75MHz is higher than the 66MHz maximum used by equivalent Intel chips. When selecting the motherboard you always need to check that it supports the processor you intend to use, but this is especially important when using non-Intel processors. Many motherboards do in fact support system clock frequencies of 75MHz or even 83MHz, but this is by no means a universal feature.

The original Pentium processors operated from a single 3.3 volt supply, but the Intel MMX chips require an additional supply potential of 2.8 volts. This second potential is known as the core voltage, and is used to power most of the chip. The 3.3-volt supply is still needed to power the parts of the chip that connect to the outside world. The alternative processors from other manufacturers also require dual supply potentials, but the additional supply potential is not necessarily 2.8 volts. For some of the Cyrix/IBM chips for example, the second supply voltage is 2.9 volts. There are several other core voltages in use, and some motherboards can provide half a dozen or more core potentials.

Unfortunately, some processors exist in more than one

version, with early examples perhaps using a different system clock frequency to later versions. With many non-Intel chips the required clock frequencies and supply voltages are marked on the top of the chip itself. It is a good idea to check that the voltages and frequencies suggested in the motherboard's manual agree with those on the processor itself. Where there is any discrepancy you must configure the motherboard to provide the operating conditions stated on the processor and not those suggested in the motherboard's manual.

It is advisable to fit the microprocessor and memory modules before fitting the motherboard into the case. Fitting memory modules is dealt with in the chapter that covers memory matters, and this aspect of things will not be considered further here. Fitting the processor was also covered earlier, and with Socket 7 chips there should be no problem provided you remember to raise the lever to the vertical position first, and get the orientation of the processor correct. The processor should then easily drop into place, and returning the lever to the horizontal position should securely lock it in place. Slot 1 processors are more like memory modules than conventional processors, and should easily fit into their sockets. They are polarised, and will only fit into the socket the right way around.

The processor's heatsink and fan should also be fitted at this stage. With Socket 7 chips, fitting the heatsink and fan can be rather fiddly and in some cases you may find that the heatsink does not clip securely in place. The side-on view of Figure 6.6 shows the simple method of fixing used for most heatsinks. With some combinations of heatsink and processor it is a rather tight fit, but once the heatsink is actually in place it should stay there and work efficiently. If the heatsink is a loose fit it may not work very well, and there is a real risk that before long it will become dislodged. If you look carefully at the clip which secures it to the motherboard, you will probably find that part of the clip can be removed and repositioned further up the main section of the clip. Using this second position should result in the heatsink and fan being held in place much more securely.

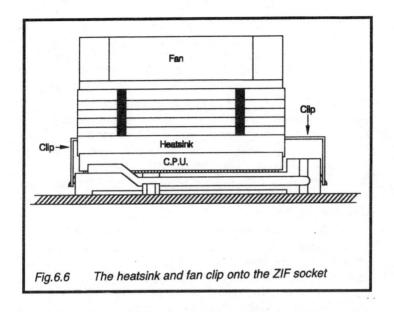

Fig.6.6   The heatsink and fan clip onto the ZIF socket

Once the board has been configured, and the processor and memory modules have been fitted, the motherboard can be mounted on the chassis. There should be no difficulty in using the old fixings with the new board, and fitting the new motherboard is generally easier than removing the old one. Any drives that were removed to enable the change of motherboard should then be reinstalled in the case, and any new drives should also be fitted at this stage. Depending on the vintage of the computer, the drives will either fit direct into the drive bays, or they will have to be fitted with plastic guide-rails first. The plastic guide-rails seem to be difficult to obtain these days, which can make life difficult when adding new drives to an old computer. You may find one or two sets of rails if you search through the odds and ends supplied with the computer, but if not there will probably no option but to improvise something. Pieces of balsa wood are easily cut to a suitable shape and will do the job quite well. Hard disc drives and CD-ROM drives are often supplied with a set of four fixing screws, but if not you will probably find some spares in the odds and ends supplied with the computer.

The next task is to fit the expansion cards and the connectors for the serial and parallel ports. It is likely that one or more of the expansion cards used in the original PC will not be needed for the upgraded version. Modern motherboards have all the normal interfaces included on the board, including such things as the serial and parallel ports, the hard and floppy disc interfaces, and on more recent boards even one or two USB ports. Expansion cards that only duplicate functions provided by the motherboard are not needed in the upgraded PC, and fitting them could prevent the PC from operating properly. If it is very difficult or impossible to fit the expansion cards in place, the motherboard is probably slightly out of position. Slightly loosen the motherboard's mounting screws, fit one of the cards in place, shifting the motherboard fractionally if necessary, and then tighten the screws again. The manual for the motherboard will include a diagram that identifies the ISA, PCI, and AGP expansion slots, but there is no risk of fitting a card in the wrong type of slot because they use connectors of different sizes.

You may find that there are connectors for the parallel and serial ports already fitted to the case, complete with "flying" leads. Where connectors are already fitted on the case, and the leads are long enough to reach the corresponding connectors on the motherboard, it is best to use the existing connectors. There should be no problem if these connectors are not present on the case, or if the leads are too short. A basic set of connecting leads and connectors should be supplied with the new motherboard. The connectors are mounted on blanking plates that can be fitted at the rear of the case behind any unused expansion slots. If there are any connectors of this type already fitted to the case, it is probably best to remove them and use the connectors supplied with the motherboard instead. There will almost certainly be too few existing connectors for all the ports on the motherboard. In addition to connectors for two serial ports and one parallel type, there is usually a connector and lead for a mouse port and (possibly) a USB port, although the latter tends to be an optional extra. It is advisable to fit and connect the connector for the mouse port even if you will be using a serial mouse. You may wish to use the mouse port at some time in the future, and it costs nothing to add it in now.

Seeing Red
There are quite a few connecting cables in the average PC, and getting everything connected correctly deters many would-be PC upgraders. Getting everything connected properly is actually much easier than you might expect. If you look at the connectors on the motherboard for the parallel ports, disc interfaces, etc., you will probably find that each connector has a pin that is marked as pin "1". This marking is also present on the data connectors of most drives, including the CD-ROM and floppy varieties. The manuals for your computer components should also have diagrams that show the pin numbering for each connector. If you look at the cables supplied with the motherboard, and those of the original PC, you will notice that they are made from grey "ribbon" cable. This type of cable always has a red line running down one side of the cable, and the convention is for this to carry the pin one connection. In order to get all the ribbon cables connected correctly you merely have to ensure that the red leads always connect to the pin one end of the connectors on the drives and motherboard. In theory, the connectors are all polarised anyway, giving no possibility of connecting them the wrong way round. In practice the connectors are often somewhat cut-down and simplified versions of the "real thing", and reverse connection is possible. Therefore, always check carefully that both ends of every cable conforms to the "red to pin one" convention.

The chapter that covers floppy disc drives explains the reason for the "twisted" floppy drive cable and you should consult this if you are unsure about the right method of connection. The IDE interfaces on modern motherboards seem to cause a certain amount of confusion, and it is important to bear in mind that each IDE interface can support two drives. The two interfaces are sometimes just referred to as IDE1 and IDE2, in other places you will find them respectively called the primary and secondary IDE interfaces. The two drives connected to each interface are the master and slave devices. Of course, you do not need to have two devices connected to each one, or indeed any IDE devices connected at all. However, a modern PC normally has at least two IDE drives, which are the hard disc and the CD-ROM drive. The hard disc drive will normally be the master device on the primary IDE interface (IDE1).

The IDE cable supplied with the motherboard invariably has provision for two drives, and the CD-ROM drive can therefore be wired-up to the second connector on this cable. It then becomes the primary slave device. In theory at any rate, it could be advantageous to have the CD-ROM drive on the secondary IDE interface. This could give faster data transfers from the CD-ROM drive to the hard disc. The problem with this method is that it requires a second IDE data cable. These are readily available from computer component suppliers. In most cases it will not be necessary to buy one, as you will probably have one left over from the original PC. I would not be inclined to bother buying an IDE cable to permit the CD-ROM drive to operate on the secondary IDE channel, but if you have a spare one you may as well use it for this purpose. It is quite likely that any CD-ROM drive in the original PC connected to an IDE interface on the sound card. If this was the case, it is best to connect the CD-ROM drive to the motherboard in the upgraded PC and leave the interface on the sound card unused. If possible, disable the IDE interface on the sound card. If the CD-ROM drive has something other than a standard IDE interface, you will need to include the relevant interface card in the upgraded PC. Again, where possible, disable any parts of the card that are not needed in the "new" PC.

Unlike PC floppy drives, the IDE drives are set as the master or slave devices via jumpers on the drives, and not by way of a "twisted" cable. CD-ROM drives normally have jumper settings for master and slave operation, plus a third called something like cable select. In a PC context it is only the master and slave options that are of interest. Hard disc drives sometimes have the same options, but there are often two master settings. One setting is used if the drive is the only device on that IDE interface, and the other is used if there is also a slave device on that IDE channel. It is best to read the manuals carefully and then set the jumpers accordingly, rather than jumping to conclusions and possibly getting things wrong.

There is still plenty to do once the drives and external interface connectors have been wired up. The power supply unit must be connected to the motherboard, and to any disc drives that are not already wired to the supply. The two power supply connectors for the motherboard are polarised, and can not be connected the wrong way round. However, they can be accidentally swapped over. The convention is for the four ground (0 volt) connections to be in the middle of the row of twelve terminals on the motherboard. With the two plugs connected correctly the four black leads should be in the middle of the group. If there are two black leads at each end of the row, the two power supply connectors have been swapped over. If you should switch on the computer with the two power connectors in this state it is unlikely that any damage will result, because the supply's protection circuit will detect the problem and it will fail to switch on. Despite this, it is better to get things right first time and not to put fail-safe systems to the test. If you are using an ATX motherboard and power supply there will be just one lead and connector, and the latter will only fit the right way round.

There will be various "flying" leads coming from LEDs, switches, and the loudspeaker mounted on the case. There will also be various connectors on the motherboard to accommodate this sort of thing. The chances of the facilities offered by the motherboard matching up with those provided by the case are pretty remote. A PC that is more than a few years old will almost certainly have a "turbo" switch and indicator LED. This facility is not normally included on modern motherboards, which always operate at maximum speed. Strangely, where a facility of this type is available, the "fine print" in the motherboard's manual usually explains that the "turbo" switch

137

does not have any effect! In some cases it is possible to use the "turbo" LED for other purposes. For example, some motherboards include a temperature sensor that monitors the temperature of the processor, and there is sometimes an output for a warning LED that will flash on and off if the processor exceeds a certain threshold temperature. In most cases though, there will be no useful function for the "turbo" LED and switch, and they will simply be left unused.

With these minor functions it is really just a matter of implementing any that are common to both the motherboard and the case, and leaving any others unconnected. This usually means connecting the power on/off indicator and IDE activity LEDs, the loudspeaker, and the reset switch, and ignoring anything else. The LEDs will only work if they are connected with the right polarity. There may be "+" markings on the leads and the motherboard to indicate the polarity, but these are often missing. If necessary you can adopt the "suck it and see" method. The LEDs will not light up if they are connected with the wrong polarity, but they will not be damaged either. If you wish to play audio CDs in the CD-ROM drive through the loudspeakers connected to the sound card, the audio output socket of the CD-ROM drive must be connected to the audio input connector of the sound card. CD-ROM drives are usually supplied complete with an audio cable that is suitable for most sound cards. Of course, if you will only play audio CDs into headphones connected to the CD-ROM drive's headphone socket, or do not intend to use the drive for audio CDs at all, this cable is not required.

Blast-Off

With everything installed in the case and the cabling completed, it is time to give everything a final check before reconnecting the monitor, mouse and keyboard, and switching on. At switch-on the computer should go through the usual BIOS start-up routine, but this routine will probably be slightly different to the one performed by the original computer. This is due to the change of BIOS that accompanied the change to a new motherboard. It is advisable to break into the start-up routine and run the BIOS Setup program before the computer tries to boot-up. A modern BIOS is very good at detecting the hardware present in the computer and adjusting itself accordingly. The user still has to set a few things manually in order to ensure correct operation of the computer. The next chapter includes an in-depth look at modern BIOS settings, and this aspect of things will not be considered in detail here.

You will need to go into the part of the Setup program that deals with the standard BIOS settings, and here you must set the correct IDE and floppy drive types. If you do not know the correct parameters for the hard disc drive this will probably not matter. The "Auto" option will get the BIOS to read the correct settings from the drive and configure itself correctly. It will probably be possible to set the time and date from the operating system once the computer is fully operational, but while you are in the standard BIOS part of the Setup program you might as well take the opportunity to set these. Once the standard CMOS settings have been dealt with it is likely that the computer will work quite well, but it might be necessary to go into the section that deals with memory settings in order to get things to work at optimum efficiency. However, in most cases you will not need to bother with this, because the BIOS will detect the memory and set the appropriate operating conditions. You can alter the defaults for things like the printer port's operating mode, and whether Num Lock is on or off at switch-on, but in most cases the standard CMOS settings are the only ones that you must set up correctly before the computer will work.

If you have not changed the hard disc drive, once you have saved and exited from the Setup program the computer will boot more or less normally. If you are using MS-DOS or MS-DOS and Windows 3.1 the computer will almost certainly boot up normally. There may be something in the AUTOEXEC.BAT or CONFIG.SYS file that does not match the new hardware configuration, so there could be one or two error messages during boot-up. If there has been a change of video card this will prevent Windows 3.1 from operating, as it will not have the correct video drivers installed. The Windows Setup program must be run and the new drivers (as supplied with the video card) installed first. Windows 3.1 should then run as before, but (hopefully) very much faster. Note that any MS-DOS programs that ran in something other than one of the standard video modes might also fail to work properly with the new video card unless you install suitable drivers first. Unfortunately, support for MS-DOS programs is waning, and there may be no option but to operate MS-DOS programs in a standard screen mode such as the 640 x 480 pixel resolution VGA mode.

With Windows 95 and 98 the computer will start to boot-up in the usual fashion, but the "plug-n-play" feature will soon start to detect the hardware changes and load the appropriate drivers. In some cases it may have suitable drivers available already, but you will usually have to put the appropriate drivers disc into the floppy or CD-ROM drive when prompted by the on-screen Windows messages. It may be necessary to use the Windows 95 or 98 CD-ROM at some stage in the proceedings, so have this disc handy just in case. Read the installation instructions provided with the various items of hardware that you have bought for the upgraded PC. Most hardware does things in standard Windows fashion, and apart from providing the drivers disc when prompted, you have to do nothing more than sit back and watch while Windows gets on with it. Some hardware requires additional installation though, and there may also be some useful utility software on the discs that has to be installed separately.

On the face of it, the only hardware that will need new drivers is the video card, plus any other expansion cards that have been changed, such as a new sound card perhaps. It can therefore be rather puzzling when Windows 95 or 98 starts reporting all manner of new hardware, and announces that it is finding and loading new software to support this hardware. In some cases it is simply rediscovering old hardware, and loading drivers that are already there. Windows 95 seems to be especially prone to this problem. Unfortunately, you often seem to end up with a PC that has two sets of drivers, neither of which are working properly. Normally the only solution to this problem is to go into the control panel, select System and then Device Manager, and then delete both versions of the offending driver. Next exit Windows and re-boot the computer. When the operating system starts to load it should detect the "new" hardware and load the drivers for it. You may not have to provide it with the drivers disc, as it may well find that it already has the necessary files on the hard disc, and reinstall them from there.

In addition to drivers for any new expansion cards, Windows will load drivers for new hardware on the motherboard. These drivers accommodate such things as improved hard disc and parallel ports, and the USB port. The computer will probably re-boot two or three times as part of the installation process, but you should eventually end up with the Windows desktop displayed on the screen, and the computer ready to run your applications. It is worth going into the Device Manager and checking that none of the hardware entries are marked with the dreaded exclamation marks, which indicate that all is not well. If there is a problem with one or more of the drivers, I usually find that deleting the offending driver or drivers and re-booting the computer clears the problem. During the re-boot the drivers are reinstalled, and they normally reinstall correctly. With an awkward PC it may take several attempts before everything installs correctly, and I assume that in some cases the drivers will only coexist peacefully if they are installed in a certain order.

One piece of hardware that may refuse to install correctly is the USB port. If you are using an early version of Windows 95 it will not have USB support, and the USB port will be unusable unless you upgrade to Windows 98. With Windows 95 OSR2 you will probably find that the USB port has an entry in Device Manager, but that there is an exclamation mark against it, and the port will not work properly. Again, the only way of getting the USB port to operate properly is to upgrade the operating system to Windows 98. The exclamation mark will then miraculously disappear, and you should find that the USB port functions perfectly. With the final version of Windows 95 (OSR2.1) you might obtain perfect results with the USB port, but there is still a possibility of erratic operation. If USB support is needed it is probably best to upgrade the operating system to Windows 98.

If the PC has been fitted with a new hard disc drive you have what is effectively a new computer, and the operating system will have to be loaded onto the hard disc before it can be used. This process is covered in the next chapter, which deals with building PCs "from scratch".

Budget Upgrades

Many people own PCs that are too old to be of any real use any more, and are not worthy of an expensive upgrade, but they do not which to simply dump them on the nearest scrap heap. The rapid rate of change in the PC world does provide an alternative in the form of a budget upgrade. Buying the current technology is not necessarily that expensive, particularly if you opt for something less than the fastest up-to-the-minute components. Buying last year's technology is even cheaper, but last year's technology is still quite fast. We are now reaching the stage where the ultimate in modern PCs is starting to provide overkill for many applications. Games enthusiasts and those who deal with complex graphics need a very fast computer. For general office applications a fairly modest Pentium PC is usually perfectly adequate, and a computer of this type is even likely to be good enough things such as 2-D computer aided design (CAD) and basic desktop publishing (DTP).

In essence a budget upgrade is not much different to an upgrade to the latest specification. It will be necessary to replace the motherboard, processor, memory modules, video card, and probably the hard disc drive as well. The difference is that you buy surplus components that are not exactly new, but have probably never been used. The large mail order companies sometimes have sales of surplus stock, but local computer fairs are probably the best source for items of this type. Inevitably, some of the items on offer at these fairs are better bargains than are others, and you certainly have to be careful not to buy a "lemon". There is no point in buying something like an ultra-cheap motherboard that only takes 60MHz and 66MHz Pentium processors if you cannot obtain a processor to fit the board, or you can only obtain one as a spare part at a high price. The better buys are often in the form of an old Pentium processor fitted on a suitable motherboard, possibly complete with some memory, a heatsink and fan, or a video card. For a modest outlay it is often possible to upgrade an old PC to a specification that will run most modern software remarkably well.

Overclocking
Overclocking is sometimes referred to as the "free upgrade", and it is the practice of using electronic components beyond their maximum speed rating. It is sometimes used with motherboards that have 75MHz and 83MHz system frequencies, but chipsets that are only rated to operate at a maximum frequency of 66MHz. The motherboard's instruction manual will usually contain one or two disclaimers, saying something along the lines that the board has the ability to use overclocking, but the manufacturer does not condone this practice. This may seem rather two-faced, but the manufacturer is basically saying that the board has the overclocking facility, but you use it at your own risk. Overclocking the motherboard's chipset is unlikely to damage anything, but good reliability can not be guaranteed.

Some non-Intel processors require the use of system frequencies of 75 or 83MHz, and this means that with some motherboards they can only be accommodated using overclocking. With other motherboards the chipset is guaranteed to operate properly at these higher clock rates. Some motherboards simply can not operate at system frequencies in excess of 66MHz, and are unusable with certain non-Intel chips even though they can handle the correct voltages and processor clock frequency. It is sometimes possible to use overclocking of the chipset to obtain a small increase in performance. For example, a processor clock frequency of 166MHz can be achieved using 66MHz x 2.5, or 83MHz x 2. Running the motherboard at 83MHz should give some increase in performance compared to 66MHz operation, even though the processor is operating at the same frequency in each case. Unfortunately, not all processors will work if the ratio of the system clock frequency to the processor clock frequency is incorrect. Intel processors seem to be the most accommodating in this respect.

Overclocking can also be applied to some microprocessors. It is only likely to be effective with processors that are made in two speeds that are essentially the same chip. For example, the Intel 166MHz and 200MHz MMX Pentium chips are the same, but the 200MHz chip is tested to higher standards and it guaranteed to work at 200MHz. Although the 166MHz chip is not guaranteed to operate at 200MHz reliably, that is not to say that it can not do so. I experimentally tried using two 166MHz MMX Pentium chips at 200MHz, and one 75MHz Pentium processor at 90MHz, and all worked perfectly for extended periods. On the other hand, two 133MHz Pentium chips refused to work at anything more than a clock frequency of 133MHz.

When trying any overclocking technique you need to bear in mind that the increased clock frequency will produce increased power consumption and heat generation. It is unlikely that any chips will overheat if their clock frequency is increased slightly, and it is very unlikely that they will function properly if their clock frequency is increased by a large amount. Therefore, overheating is not a major worry, but if a fault should occur when you are using a component beyond its normal maximum operating frequency it will not be covered by the guarantee. If you experiment with overclocking, you do so at your own risk.

Chapter 7

DIY PCs

With a vast number of ready made PCs available there may seem to be no point in building your own, but there can be real advantages in the DIY approach. When choosing a new PC most people seek out a computer that has most of the features they require at a price they can afford. It usually requires a great deal of searching, but in the end most people find something that more or less suits their needs at a price they can afford. Rather than searching all the adverts for a PC that has the right specification at the right price, why not select the individual components that best suit your needs and assemble them into a complete PC? You can then have your ideal PC with no compromises other than those enforced by financial constraints.

Many people try their hand at DIY PC construction in an attempt to save money. Provided you purchase the individual components wisely it is likely that there will be a small cost saving. However, do not expect to get a half price PC by building it yourself. A saving of around 10 percent is certainly quite possible, and with careful buying you may even achieve a saving of as much as 20 percent. On the other hand, with imprudent buying you could easily end up paying 10 or 20 percent more for your PC. Assembling a PC takes no more than a very few hours work, and it would be unrealistic to expect the DIY approach to produce massive savings. It is probably not the assembly costs that account for the majority of the savings anyway. When you buy a new PC it generally comes complete with some sort of support package such as a one-year onsite maintenance contract and some sort of telephone support system.

When building your own PC you have the individual guarantees for the various components that you buy, and in some cases there may well be some form of telephone support as well. What you lack is any form of overall support for the system, and if things go wrong it is largely up to you to sort them out yourself. This lack of support is unlikely to be of importance if you have a few years experience at dealing with PCs. The chances are that you would not bother using a support line even if one were available. You would just do what you always do, and sort out the problem yourself. The lack of any onsite maintenance contract is probably a larger drawback for most people, and if something should go wrong with the computer it could take some while to obtain a replacement component. Of course, you may be able to negotiate an onsite maintenance contract for your DIY PC by dealing direct with one of the companies that provide this service. Understandably, they might not be interested in providing support for PC that has not been produced by one of the major computer manufacturers. Even if they will provide support the cost could be very high. DIY PCs are most suitable for those who have some experience at dealing with PC matters, and will not be wholly reliant on the finished computer. If you will only use the PC for leisure or occasional business use, or you have a second PC that you can use in emergencies, DIY PCs are a reasonably safe option.

Kitted Out
The main advantage of building your own PC is that you can select the components that best suit your needs. First you need to carefully consider what uses the computer will be put to, so that you can determine the areas where compromises can be safely made, and those where high performance is essential. If the computer will be used for the latest games it is essential to choose a graphics card that offers top-quality 3-D performance. A fast processor and plenty of memory would also be a decided asset. Obviously 3-D graphics performance is of little or no importance for a computer that will be used for 2-D graphics applications such as photographic image manipulation or DTP. It is then the 2-D graphics performance that is of most importance and a fairly large monitor may also be required. For general business applications a "bog standard" video card and processor will probably be more than adequate.

146

Probably the best way of handing things is to make a list of all the components required for the finished PC, complete with brief notes detailing any special requirements. It is then a matter of studying reviews in computer magazines and looking through magazine advertisements in order to find the best components at a price you can afford. If your aim is merely to produce a PC at a "rock bottom" price it becomes more matter of scanning the advertisements for "special offers" and touring the local computer fairs for the best deals you can obtain. Either way, this list represents the minimum you will require in order to produce a working PC.

Case with PSU, set of fixing screws, etc.
Motherboard with cables, etc.
Memory modules to suit the motherboard
Microprocessor with matching heatsink and fan
Keyboard and mouse
Video card
Monitor
3.5 inch floppy disc drive
Hard disc drive
CD-ROM drive

The CD-ROM drive is not strictly necessary, but as most software is supplied on CD-ROMs these days you will probably not get far without one. For multimedia applications, voice recognition, etc., you will also require a sound card and speakers plus (possibly) a headset and microphone. You may also require other items such as a printer and a modem, but here we will only consider the main constituent parts of the PC itself. It is advisable to put together a basic PC and get it working, and then add peripherals such as scanners, printers, and modems.

Although the obvious starting point when selecting the components used is to choose the processor and motherboard, I would suggest choosing the processor and video card first, and then choosing a motherboard to suit them. This is simply because there are now so many different processors available that no motherboard will operate with all of them. You therefore have to choose the processor first, and then select from the particular motherboards that will operate with that processor. If you choose a video card that fits a PCI expansion slot it should be compatible with any motherboard. The same is not true if you select a video card that requires an AGP (advanced graphics port) expansion slot. This form of expansion bus is increasingly common, but is by no means a universal motherboard feature. If you choose an AGP video card you must make sure that you obtain a motherboard that has a suitable expansion slot.

As explained in the previous chapter, motherboards are available with two different form factors. These are the AT and ATX varieties, and the former generally costs somewhat less than the latter. When building "from scratch" you are obviously not tied in to one type or other, and you can choose whichever you feel is best. Although the AT variety is somewhat cheaper, the ATX layout seems likely to become the "standard" in the not too distant future. Even now, there are more ATX style motherboards than AT types available. I would therefore be inclined to opt for an ATX motherboard, power supply, and case, as this would seem to be better future-proofed. Most modern AT style motherboards can actually be used in an ATX case, but if you are going to use an ATX case there would seem to be no point in fitting it with an AT motherboard. The best style of case to use (desktop, full tower, etc.) is obviously a matter of personal preference, but for a DIY PC I would advise against using any form of small case. The very limited amount of space inside such a case can make the PC very difficult to work on, and with some of them it can be very difficult to get the motherboard into place. Medium and large cases are much easier to work on, and also provide plenty of space for disc drives, CD-ROM drives, etc.

It is best to leave the choice of keyboard until you have obtained the motherboard. There are two types of keyboard connector, which are the five-way DIN type and the smaller PS/2 variety. In the past it was mainly the five-way DIN type that was

148

Probably the best way of handing things is to make a list of all the components required for the finished PC, complete with brief notes detailing any special requirements. It is then a matter of studying reviews in computer magazines and looking through magazine advertisements in order to find the best components at a price you can afford. If your aim is merely to produce a PC at a "rock bottom" price it becomes more matter of scanning the advertisements for "special offers" and touring the local computer fairs for the best deals you can obtain. Either way, this list represents the minimum you will require in order to produce a working PC.

Case with PSU, set of fixing screws, etc.
Motherboard with cables, etc.
Memory modules to suit the motherboard
Microprocessor with matching heatsink and fan
Keyboard and mouse
Video card
Monitor
3.5 inch floppy disc drive
Hard disc drive
CD-ROM drive

The CD-ROM drive is not strictly necessary, but as most software is supplied on CD-ROMs these days you will probably not get far without one. For multimedia applications, voice recognition, etc., you will also require a sound card and speakers plus (possibly) a headset and microphone. You may also require other items such as a printer and a modem, but here we will only consider the main constituent parts of the PC itself. It is advisable to put together a basic PC and get it working, and then add peripherals such as scanners, printers, and modems.

Although the obvious starting point when selecting the components used is to choose the processor and motherboard, I would suggest choosing the processor and video card first, and then choosing a motherboard to suit them. This is simply because there are now so many different processors available that no motherboard will operate with all of them. You therefore have to choose the processor first, and then select from the particular motherboards that will operate with that processor. If you choose a video card that fits a PCI expansion slot it should be compatible with any motherboard. The same is not true if you select a video card that requires an AGP (advanced graphics port) expansion slot. This form of expansion bus is increasingly common, but is by no means a universal motherboard feature. If you choose an AGP video card you must make sure that you obtain a motherboard that has a suitable expansion slot.

As explained in the previous chapter, motherboards are available with two different form factors. These are the AT and ATX varieties, and the former generally costs somewhat less than the latter. When building "from scratch" you are obviously not tied in to one type or other, and you can choose whichever you feel is best. Although the AT variety is somewhat cheaper, the ATX layout seems likely to become the "standard" in the not too distant future. Even now, there are more ATX style motherboards than AT types available. I would therefore be inclined to opt for an ATX motherboard, power supply, and case, as this would seem to be better future-proofed. Most modern AT style motherboards can actually be used in an ATX case, but if you are going to use an ATX case there would seem to be no point in fitting it with an AT motherboard. The best style of case to use (desktop, full tower, etc.) is obviously a matter of personal preference, but for a DIY PC I would advise against using any form of small case. The very limited amount of space inside such a case can make the PC very difficult to work on, and with some of them it can be very difficult to get the motherboard into place. Medium and large cases are much easier to work on, and also provide plenty of space for disc drives, CD-ROM drives, etc.

It is best to leave the choice of keyboard until you have obtained the motherboard. There are two types of keyboard connector, which are the five-way DIN type and the smaller PS/2 variety. In the past it was mainly the five-way DIN type that was used, and this is still the normal form of keyboard connector for AT motherboards. Most ATX style motherboards seem to have PS/2 keyboard connectors, and you must therefore be careful to obtain a compatible keyboard if you opt for an ATX motherboard.

A mouse port now seems to be a standard motherboard feature, and you therefore have the choice of either a serial mouse or a mouse port type. Serial mice are by far the most popular, but a mouse port mouse has the advantage of leaving the serial port free for other purposes. Although mouse ports have a reputation for causing problems, these mainly occur when using a mouse port device with the computer that previously used a serial mouse. When building a new computer I have never experienced any difficulties with them.

Bits and Pieces

In addition to the main components of the PC you will need various bits and pieces such as mounting bolts for the motherboard and drives, and connecting cables. The case and power supply are normally supplied with fixing screws for the motherboard, expansion cards, and disc drives. The motherboard should be supplied with a basic set of cables and connectors for the drives and ports. Depending on your requirements and the cables supplied, it might be necessary to purchase one or two additional leads.

Before installing the motherboard in the case it should be fitted with the memory modules, plus the microprocessor together with its heatsink and cooling fan. Fitting the processor and memory modules has been covered in previous chapters and will not be covered again here. Neither will the warnings about static-sensitive components, and the advice about handling them safely. When working on the motherboard I would recommend using an earthed worktop, using a piece of aluminium foil in the manner described in the previous chapter. The case and power supply unit can be used to provide an earthing point for the foil, but remember to make sure that the power is switched off at both the mains outlet and the computer's on/off switch. Where appropriate, remember to set the jumpers or DIP-switches to configure the motherboard to suit the processor that you are using.

The motherboard must be mounted on the base of the case in such a way that the connections on the underside of the board are held well clear of the metal case. Otherwise the connections will short circuit to earth, and it is possible that the motherboard could be damaged. The case should be supplied complete with any additional odds and ends that are needed to mount the motherboard properly. Some cases have metal stand-offs already fixed in place, while others require the user to fit them. They may need to be bolted in place using screws that are fitted from the underside of the case, but these days it seems to be more common for simple clip-in types to be used. These just push into cut-outs in the base of the case, but they often need a fair amount of force before they will clip into place. It is still quite common for a mixture of metal and plastic stand-offs to be used. The tops of the stand-offs are pushed into the appropriate holes in the motherboard so that the stand-offs are fitted on the underside of the board. The board assembly then slides into position, with the bottoms of the stand-offs fitting into guides in the base panel of the case. Fixing screws are then used to secure the motherboard to the metal stand-offs. You are unlikely to get any assembly instructions supplied with the case, so it is a matter of examining the case and the various bits of hardware provided with it, and using some common sense to determine how everything fits together.

Once the motherboard is correctly installed in the case the disc drives can be fitted. Modern cases do not require the drives to be fitted with plastic guide-rails, and there should be no difficulty in sliding then into the drive bays. The fancy fascias of some cases make it necessary to fit the drives from the rear and slide them forwards into position. With most cases you can fit them from the front, which is usually very much easier. With the 5.25 in. drives there will probably be provision for four mounting bolts each side, but two each side will be sufficient to secure the drives firmly in place. The construction of some cases is such that one side of at least one drive may be inaccessible. Some

150

dismantling of the case may provide access so that the fixing screws can be fitted, but there are unlikely to be any problems if you only fit the mounting screws in one side of a drive. With one of two cases I have encountered you do not have any choice in this matter!

The motherboard should be supplied complete with a basic set of connecting cables. For an ATX board this will probably just be floppy drive and IDE data cables. Both of these cables will support two drives, but in the case of the IDE drives you may prefer to buy a second cable so that the hard disc and the CD-ROM drive can be operated from separate IDE ports. If you settle for a single cable the drives can be connected to the IDE1 or the IDE2 interface, but the convention is to use the IDE1 port. If you are unsure about the correct method of connecting the floppy drive cable, refer back to the chapter that deals with disc drives.

An AT motherboard does not have "proper" on-board connectors for the serial and parallel ports. Instead, the basic connectors on the board are wired to sockets mounted on the rear of the case or in blanking plates that are fitted behind any vacant expansion slots. The board should be supplied with connectors and leads for the serial and parallel ports, and possibly connectors and leads for the mouse port as well. These connectors are normally mounted in blanking plates, but it is usually quite easy to remove them from the plates and mount them on the case. At the ends of each connector there are two hexagonal threaded bushes, which accept the screws on the serial and parallel leads. These can be unscrewed with the aid of a pair of pliers, and the connectors should then readily pull free from the blanking plates. They can then be mounted on the rear of the case using the screws that have just been removed to bolt them back in place. Unless there is a shortage of vacant expansion slots I simply leave the connectors on the blanking plates. One potential problem with repositioning them on the case is that you might find that the "flying" leads will not reach to the connectors on the motherboard.

Getting the data cables connected around the right way is not usually too difficult because many of the connectors are polarised and will only fit the right way round. Unfortunately, the connectors on the motherboard are often very basic, and the data cables sometimes lack the polarising key anyway. You then have to look at the drives and the motherboard in search of pin numbers for the various connectors. If these numbers are not marked on the various pieces of hardware, details of the pin numbering should be provided in the instruction manuals. The data cables are normally made from grey "ribbon" cable, but the lead at one end of the cable is coloured red, and the convention is for this to carry the pin one connection. If you ensure that the "red" end of the connectors on the cables always connect to the pin 1 ends of the connectors on the drives and motherboard, everything will connect together correctly.

The power supply connectors for the disc drives are polarised, and you will be unable to fit them the wrong way around even if you try. In fact the larger connectors for the 5.25-in. drives can be quite difficult to connect the right way round, and will probably require very firm pressure. The smaller connectors for 3.5 in. drives are much easier to deal with, but if you are using a 3.5-in. hard disc drive do not be surprised if it actually uses the larger size of power connector. An ATX power supply has a single cable and connector to carry power to the motherboard. Polarised connectors are used, so you can only connect the supply with the correct polarity. An AT power supply has two cables that connect to the motherboard. These are fitted with polarised but identical connectors, making it possible to get them swapped over. The convention is for the four ground (0 volt) terminals to be grouped in the middle of the line of 12. Black leads in the power supply cables normally carry the ground connections, and if the cables are connected properly the four black leads should therefore be grouped together and not at opposite ends.

The processor's cooling fan requires a 12-volt supply, and it might be fitted with a connector that enables this supply to be obtained from the motherboard. Any modern motherboard should have two small terminals near the processor that are specifically intended to power the cooling fan. There should be a layout diagram in the motherboard's manual that shows the position of this supply output. Most processor cooling fans do not actually have this type of connector, but are instead designed to take power from one of the power supply outputs for a 5.25-in. disc drive. There will also be an output cable and connector that can be used to carry the supply through to a disc drive. Therefore, even if there is no spare 5.25-in. drive supply cable you can still tap off power for the cooling fan.

On the Cards
To complete the computer the expansion cards are added and any remaining cables are connected. Fitting the cards should not be difficult provided the motherboard is positioned accurately in the case. If the expansion cards are reluctant to fit into position, loosen the mounting bolts for the motherboard slightly and then try to fit one of the cards. If necessary, shift the motherboard slightly so that the card can fit into position. Once one of the cards is in place, the mounting bolts for the motherboard can be re-tightened, and the remaining cards should then fit into position quite easily.

There will be several "flying" leads emanating from the case and to a large extent these should match up with terminals on the motherboard. The chances of the facilities offered by the case matching those of the motherboard are remote. For example, there are still cases that have a "turbo" switch and indicator LED, but it is unlikely that the motherboard will support two-speed operation. A few motherboards do actually have terminals for the "turbo" switch and LED, but the manual politely explains that they do not actually have any real purpose. The motherboard operates at full speed regardless of the setting of the "turbo" switch. It is really just a matter of connecting together any facilities that are common to both the case and the motherboard. This usually means the power and IDE activity LEDs, the loudspeaker, and the reset switch. If the motherboard has something like an output for a processor overheating warning LED, it might be possible to use this to drive the "turbo" LED, but in most cases any "turbo" LED or switch will simply have to be left unused. There are sometimes "+" signs to indicate the correct polarity when connecting LEDs to the motherboard, but in most cases the polarity markings will be absent on either the motherboard or the leads. It is then just a matter of using trial and error to find the correct method of connection. Connecting the LEDs with the wrong polarity will not do them any harm.

These days most CD-ROM drives are supplied complete with an audio cable that can connect the audio output at the rear of the drive to the audio input of the sound card. This enables audio CDs in the CD-ROM drive to play through the computer's speakers. This lead is not needed if you will only play audio CDs through headphones connected direct to the CD-ROM drive, or if you are not interested in playing audio CDs at all. On the other hand, you may as well fit it anyway just in case you need to use this facility at some future time. The connector at the sound card end of the cable will almost certainly be a type that is compatible with SoundBlaster cards. Most other sound cards now use the same type of connector, or have two audio input connectors including one SoundBlaster compatible type. There is still a slight risk that the cable will not be compatible with your sound card, and you will then have to seek out a cable of the correct type.

Final Checks
With the minor cabling completed the base unit of the computer is finished. Before connecting the mouse, keyboard, and monitor it is definitely a good idea to thoroughly check everything, making sure that all the cables are connected correctly and that none have been accidentally dislodged when working on the unit. When the computer is switched on it should go through the normal BIOS start-up routine. If nothing happens, or there is any sign of a malfunction, switch off at once and recheck the entire wiring, etc. Assuming all is well, break out of the start-up routine and enter the BIOS Setup program. The usual way of entering the Setup program is to press the "Del" key when prompted by an on-screen message.

In the original AT computers the CMOS memory was only used to store a few items of information about the hardware configuration. A modern BIOS still uses the CMOS memory to store this information, but this memory is used to store many other parameters as well. This makes setting up the BIOS a rather daunting task, and even some highly experienced computer users are apprehensive about tampering with the BIOS settings. While it is true that a modern BIOS is highly technical and that only the real hardware experts actually understand every aspect of it, it is also true to say that the DIY PC builder does not really need to get deeply involved with setting up the BIOS. The BIOS will be customised to suit the particular motherboard it is fitted on, and to a large extent it will adopt sensible defaults. You will still need to set things like the time, date, and drive types, but it will probably not be essential to alter anything else.

Most of the current motherboards are fitted with either an Award or an AMI (American Megatrends Inc.) BIOS. These offer broadly similar facilities but differ in points of detail. The AMI BIOS Setup program has mouse support, and can operate with a sort of simplified Windows method of mouse control, although it can still be controlled via the keyboard if preferred. All the Award BIOS Setup programs I have encountered so far only had provision for keyboard control, but they use a form of multiple menus to make it easy to select a parameter and modify it. Here we will use an Award BIOS Setup program to show the kinds of thing that can be controlled via the Setup program. The BIOS for your new computer will almost certainly be slightly different to the one described here, but it will probably only differ in minor ways.

Standard BIOS

There are so many parameters that can be controlled via the BIOS Setup program that they are normally divided into half a dozen or so groups. The most important of these is the "Standard CMOS Setup", which is basically the same as the BIOS Setup in the original AT style PCs. The first parameters in the list are the time and date. These can usually be set via an operating system utility these days, but you may as well set them from the Setup program while you are in that section of the program. The next section is used to set the operating parameters for the devices on the IDE ports. For the sake of this example we will assume that the hard disc is the master device on the primary IDE channel (IDE1), and that the CD-ROM is the master device on the secondary IDE channel (IDE2). If the manuals for the drives provide the correct figures to enter into the CMOS memory, and they certainly should do so in the case of hard disc drives, you can enter these figures against the appropriate device. In this case the hard disc drive is the "Primary Master". A modern AMI BIOS should have a setting specifically for a CD-ROM drive, and this can be used for the "Secondary Master" device. Simply setting everything at zero usually works where no CR-ROM setting is available. There are no primary or secondary slave drives, so simply enter "None" for these.

If you do not know the appropriate figures for your drives it does not really matter, because there is always an "Auto" option. If this is selected, the BIOS examines the hardware during the start-up routine and enters the correct figures automatically. This usually works very well, but with some drives it can take a while, which extends the boot-up time. If you go back to the initial menu you will find a section called "IDE HDD Auto Detection", and this offers a similar auto-detection facility. When this option is selected, the Setup program examines the hardware on each IDE channel, and offers suggested settings for each of the four possible IDE devices. If you accept the suggested settings for the hard disc drive (or drives) they will be entered into the CMOS RAM. After using this auto-detection facility it is a good idea to return to the "Standard CMOS Setup" page to check that the settings have been transferred correctly. Also, make sure that "None" is entered for the drive type where appropriate.

The last parameter for each IDE drive is usually something like Auto, Normal, LBA (large block addressing), and Large.

Normal is for drives under 528MB, while LBA and Large are alternative modes for drives having a capacity of more than 528MB. Modern drives have capacities of well in excess of 528MB, and mostly require the LBA mode. The manual for the hard drive should give some guidance here, or you can simply select Auto and let the BIOS sort things out for itself.

Some users get confused because they think a hard drive that will be partitioned should have separate entries in the BIOS for each partition. This is not the case, and as far as the BIOS is concerned each physical hard disc is a single drive, and has just one entry in the CMOS RAM table. The partitioning of hard discs is handled by the operating system, and so is the assignment of drive letters. The BIOS is only concerned with the physical characteristics of the drives, and not how data will be arranged and stored on the discs.

The next section in the "Standard CMOS Setup" is used to select the floppy disc drive type or types. All the standard types of floppy drive are normally supported, from the old 5.25-inch 360K drives to the rare 2.88M-3.5 inch type. You simply select the appropriate type for drives A and B. Select "None" for drive B if the computer has only one floppy drive. In days gone by you had to enter the amount of memory fitted, but with a modern BIOS the amount of memory is automatically detected and entered into the CMOS RAM. The "Standard CMOS Setup" screen will report the amount of memory fitted, and will display something like this:

Base Memory:	640K
Extended Memory:	15360K
Other Memory:	384K
Total Memory:	16384K

For those who are new to computing the way in which the amount of memory is reported can seem rather strange. It should look very familiar to those who can remember the early days of IBM compatible PCs. The original PCs had relatively simple processors that could only address one megabyte of RAM, but only the lower 640K of the address range were actually used for RAM. The upper 384K of the address range was used for the BIOS ROM, video ROM, and that sort of thing. Modern PCs can address hundreds of megabytes of RAM, but the lowest one megabyte is still arranged in much the same way that it was in the original PCs. The BIOS therefore reports that there is 640K of normal (base) memory, so many kilobytes of RAM above the original one megabyte of RAM (extended memory), and 384K of other memory. This "other" memory is the RAM in the address space used by the BIOS, etc. Note that there is no way of altering the settings reported by the BIOS. If the total amount of memory does not agree with the amount of memory you have fitted there is a memory fault. You should then switch off and check that the memory modules are all installed correctly.

The final section of the standard set-up enables the type of video card to be specified, and the degree of error trapping to be selected. The BIOS will probably detect the video card and set the appropriate type, which for a modern PC will presumably be a EGA/VGA type. You can select an old CGA or mono adapter, but these are obsolete and not used in modern PCs. The error trapping controls the way in which the computer responds to errors that are found during the BIOS self-testing routing at switch-on. The default of halt on all errors is probably the best choice, particularly when you are testing a new PC.

Setting up the standard CMOS parameters is probably all you will need to do in order to get the computer running properly, but it is a good idea to look at the options available in the other sections of the Setup program. The chipset Setup controls things such as the port and memory timing. You can "play" with these settings in an attempt to obtain improved performance, but higher speed may well produce lower reliability. Results should be quite good if you simply leave this section with the auto configuration enabled. If you are using EDO memory you might find that the DRAM Timing defaults to 70ns. This should be changed to 60ns for EDO RAM. If the PC is fitted with

SDRAM it may be necessary to set the SDRAM CAS Latency. The default setting will probably be suitable, but check in the motherboard's manual to ensure that it is at the correct figure for the system clock frequency and SDRAM speed (10 or 12ns) that you are using.

The Power Management Setup will probably be set to Disabled, and this is probably the best way to leave it. A lot of power management features can be controlled via the operating system these days, and some of the peripheral devices in the computer might not support the power management features anyway. Many of these BIOS settings would seem to be of little relevance. You may find that there are various CPU threshold temperatures that can be selected. If the CPU goes above the selected temperature a warning is produced, and the PC usually shuts down as well. Again, it is probably best to simply leave this at its default setting. You may find that the BIOS displays the current case temperature of the processor in this page of the Setup program. Anything below about 55 degrees Celsius should be completely safe.

Unless you know what you are doing it is not a good idea to mess around with the PNP/PCI settings. The defaults should work perfectly well anyway. There will be the option of selecting "Yes" when a PNP ("plug-n-play") operating system is installed or "No" when a non-PNP type is installed. Windows 95 and 98 are PNP operating systems, and the obvious setting is Yes if you will use either of these. In practice there can be problems if Yes is selected, and it is probably best to leave the default setting of No.

The Integrated Peripherals section provides some control over the on-board interfaces. In particular, it allows each port to be switched on or off, and in the case of the serial and parallel ports it also enables the port addresses and interrupt (IRQ) numbers to be altered. This can be useful when trying to avoid conflicts with hardware fitted in the expansion slots. There will be various parallel port modes available, but with a modern BIOS it is unlikely that there will be a Standard (output only) mode. The choices will probably be SPP, EPP, and ECP, which are all bi-directional modes. For most purposes either SPP or EPP will suffice. Only set ECP operation if you use the port with a device that definitely needs this mode. If the motherboard supports infrared communications it will be possible to switch serial port two (COM2) between normal operation and infrared operation. When set to infrared operation it is possible for the PC to communicate with suitably equipped notebook computers and digital cameras that support infrared communications. However, the correct hardware add-on is needed on COM2 before this cordless communications will be possible. Make sure that IDE HDD Block Mode is enabled, because the hard disc performance will be relatively poor if it is not.

The BIOS Features Setup controls some useful features, but once again the default settings should suffice. The internal and external caches must be enabled if the computer is to operate at full speed. There are various boot sequence options, and eventually you might like to select C Only. In the meantime the boot sequence must include drive A, since this is the one that the computer must boot from until drive C is made bootable. After boot-up the NumLock key is normally on, but this can be set to Off after boot-up if preferred. There are various BIOS address ranges listed, and the options of enabling or disabling shadowing of each one. By default the video BIOS will be shadowed, but the other address ranges will not. Shadowing of a BIOS is where it is copied into the computer's RAM and then run from there. The top 384K of the base memory is given over to the main BIOS, plus any other device that needs its own BIOS. In a modern PC this part of the memory map is occupied by RAM, but this RAM is normally disabled. When shadowing is enabled, the relevant block of RAM is enabled, and the contents of the BIOS at that address range are copied into it. The point of this is that the RAM is faster than the ROM used for the BIOS, and using shadowing should speed up operation of the video card. Usually the only peripheral that has its own BIOS is the video card, but shadowing of other parts of the top 384K of memory can be enabled if necessary. If you have a peripheral device that will benefit from this treatment, its manual should say so, and specify the address range that must be shadowed.

Other sections allow you to select a user password that must be entered before the PC will boot up, load the default settings, save the new settings and exit, or exit without saving any changes to the settings. Being able to load the default settings is useful if you experiment a little too much and end up with totally unsuitable settings.

Finding Fault

Once you are satisfied with the BIOS settings, save them and exit. The computer can then be booted from a MS-DOS system disc in drive A, but it can not be booted from the hard drive at this stage. Hard disc partitioning, formatting, and installing the operating system were covered in chapter 3, so refer back to chapter 3 if you are unfamiliar with this aspect of things. There can be difficulties in obtaining the Windows 98 operating system for a home constructed PC. One solution is to buy Windows 3.1 and MS-DOS, and then upgrade these to Windows 98. Alternatively you can try to purchase the full version of Windows 98, but this is not sold on its own. It should only be sold with "hardware", but apparently "hardware" does not necessarily mean a complete PC. It is legitimate for a supplier to sell you Windows 98 at the same time as you buy some major item of hardware, such as a motherboard and processor. This provides the PC user with a "get-out clause" that should enable him or her to purchase the full version of Windows 98.

If the new computer refuses to boot up, or malfunctions in some way, do not panic. Switch off and then check that all the cables are connected properly, the configuration jumpers and switches are set correctly, and that everything is as it should be. There is often quite a jumble of cables in a PC, and it is not uncommon for one cable to become dislodged while another one is being fitted. Make quite sure that all the connectors on the cables are fully pushed home into the connectors on the motherboard and the drives. When I am asked to sort out problems with newly constructed or upgraded computers the most common problem is that one of the IDE drives has not been configured correctly. In your haste to get the computer completed it is easy to overlook this type of thing. If the BIOS start-up routine seems to go on forever, and the computer behaves erratically thereafter, a configuration problem in one of the IDE drives is the most likely cause of the problem.

The chance of a problem occurring with the microprocessor are very low, because the processor will only fit onto the motherboard the right way round, and very high quality ZIF sockets are used on even the cheaper motherboards. If the processor fails to function properly the most likely cause is the motherboard being configured incorrectly. If the motherboard has some form of automatic processor detection facility, check that the right processor is specified on the initial start-up screen. If the wrong processor is identified it will be necessary to go into the appropriate section of the BIOS Setup program and set the processor parameters manually. Note that if you are using a processor that has a clock frequency that is actually lower than its "equivalent" speed rating, it is almost certainly the true clock frequency that the BIOS will use on the initial start-up screen. If the motherboard is configured via jumpers or DIP switches, check carefully against the manual for the motherboard that you are using precisely the required settings.

If the computer fails to enter the normal BIOS start-up routine at all, it is possible that there is a processor fault, but a memory problem is the more likely cause of the failure. With a major failure of this type the computer will either do nothing at all, or just make the occasional "beep" sound. Even if you have done so already, carefully check the section of the motherboard's manual that deals with memory matters. Make sure that you are using an acceptable memory arrangement, and that the motherboard is not fitted with an unacceptable mixture of memory types. Although DIMMs can usually be used in multiples of one, SIMMs normally have to be used in pairs. These days most motherboards are very flexible, but if you are only using a single DIMM or one pair of SIMMs you might have to fit the modules in the right bank of sockets for the memory to work correctly. Where the motherboard has provision for both

DIMMs and SIMMs it will probably not be possible to use all the memory sockets. In some cases a mixture of DIMMs and SIMMs is not allowed at all, and in others the DIMM holders and one pair of SIMM sockets effectively occupy the same section of memory, and you can therefore only use one of the other. When choosing the memory for a modern PC it is essential to read the "small print" in the relevant section of the motherboard's manual.

A problem with the memory is most likely to be caused by one of the memory modules not fitting into its holder correctly. The quality of holders for memory modules is often quite poor even on some of the more up-market motherboards. This tends to make it quite difficult to fit the modules into the holders, and in some cases they can be difficult to remove as well. Look carefully at the modules and make quite sure that they fit right down into the holders. When in place correctly the modules should lock into position, so try giving the modules a gentle tug to see if they pull free from the holders. If a module pulls away from its holder, even at just one end, it is not fitted in the holder correctly. Although it should not be possible to fit a SIMM the wrong way round, some SIMM holders are so low in quality that this can actually be done. If this should happen, on close inspection the module will clearly be seen to be off-centre. Whenever problems with the memory are suspected it is a good idea to remove the memory modules and re-fit them. This often seems to remove the problem.

Disc Problems
If you are using a UDMA33 hard disc drive, and the motherboard also has full UDMA33 support, it might seem reasonable to expect the hard disc to operate at full speed. In fact you will only obtain high-speed data transfers if the operating system has a UDMA33 driver loaded. In order to use this hard disc interface to full effect you will need a modern operating system that supports it properly. With Windows 98 you should find that UDMA33 support is installed automatically, but this is not the case with Windows 95. The motherboard should be supplied with a UDMA33 driver for Windows 95, together with

installation instructions. With this loaded you should find that the hard disc drive operates noticeably faster. I have never downloaded it, but the Windows 95 driver is apparently available on the Intel web site (search for the file called SETUPEX.EXE).

Newcomers to PC construction often complain that it is impossible to format the hard disc drive because MS-DOS will not recognised drive C as a valid drive letter. The normal cause of this problem is that the disc has not been partitioned using FDISC, and as far as the operating system is concerned there is no disc to format. It has to be emphasised that FDISC or some other partitioning program must be used to create a partition before the disc can be formatted. If you will need to boot from the disc you must create a primary DOS partition and transfer the system files to this disc partition. Any further disc partitions will be drives D, E, etc., and they must be formatted separately. Off course, there is no need to transfer the system files to these additional partitions.

IDE devices can sometimes be troublesome for no apparent reason. The causes of this seem to be highly technical, and apparently revolve around different manufacturers interpreting the IDE specification in slightly different ways. The practical consequence is that some IDE devices are to some degree incompatible with others. Incompatibility problems of this type are most likely to occur when using old and new drives together, but they can also occur when using a modern hard disc drive and a CD-ROM drive on the same IDE port. This usually happens when the hard disc drive is a UDMA33 type but the CD-ROM drive does not have a UDMA33 interface. The hard disc will usually function properly. The CD-ROM drive may simply fail to work at all, but it is more likely that it will behave in an erratic manner. When this type of problem occurs it is usually possible to effect a cure by operating the devices on different IDE ports.

After going through the usual installation procedure for the operating system the hard disc will use the FAT16 disc filing system. This system is not very efficient with large hard drives because it accommodates these drives by using large sectors.

In fact with modern hard disc drives the sector size will be some 32K. This may not seem to be of great practical importance, but it actually results in the great deal of wasted hard disc space. The important point here is that each sector can only be used in one file, and this means that small files will each occupy 32K of hard disc space. Even if a file only contains one byte of data it will still occupy 32K of the hard disc! Even with large files there can be a significant amount of wastage. On average the final sector used by a large file will be only half full and will waste some 16K of disc space. This means that at least 16K per file will be wasted, and because Windows application programs tend to use large numbers of small support files the actual wastage is often in excess of 20K per file.

The later versions of Windows 95 have support for an improved disc filing system called FAT32, which stores each sector address as a 32-bit number rather than a 16-bit value. This enables a sector size of just 4K to be used with large hard disc drives, giving greatly reduced wastage. Changing to the FAT32 disc filing system seems to provide an effective increase in capacity of about 20 percent or so. Support for the FAT32 filing system is something less than complete with Windows 95, and the usual way of converting the drive to FAT32 is to use a program such as Partition Magic 3.0. Things are much easier with Windows 98, which has a built-in conversion utility. This program is accessed via Start, Programs, Accessories, System Tools, and then selecting Drive Converter (FAT32). The conversion utility is very straightforward to use, but read the various warning notices before you go ahead with the conversion. Most of the potential drawbacks are minor, but if you have the computer set up for dual-boot (MS-DOS/Windows 98) operation you will find that the MS-DOS boot option is no longer available once the drive has been converted. This is simply due to the fact that FAT32 and MS-DOS are incompatible. However, the Windows 98 version of DOS will still be available by way of the MS-DOS prompt and the "reboot in MS-DOS" option on the Shutdown screen. If you boot up from a disc in drive A that contains some form of "genuine" MS-DOS, the system will not recognise any FAT32 disc partition. Note that the FDISK program supplied with Windows 98 can produce FAT32 partitions, and that it can also handle large partitions over 2.1GB.

USB!

At the time of writing this, USB ports are not used a great deal in practice, even though this type of interface has now been around for quite a while. This lack of support has probably been due to difficulties in using USB with Windows 95, but it seems likely that this type of interface will become increasing important in the future. With most versions of Windows 95 the USB port (if fitted) will appear in Device Manager, but the entry here will almost certainly be complete with an exclamation mark and warnings to the effect that the port is not present or not functioning properly. If you are using the final version of Windows 95 you may find that any USB port on the motherboard is fully installed, but there could still be problems in using it. Windows 98 has proper support for USB ports, and when using this operating system you should find that there are no major problems when using USB peripherals. Users of Windows 95 who wish to use USB ports would be well advised to upgrade to Windows 98. According to Microsoft, it is not possible to upgrade early version of Windows 95 to provide proper USB support.

Index